Confronting Racism
Teacher Education

MW00652907

ebrooksanyackschools.org

Confronting Racism in Teacher Education aims to transform systematic and persistent racism through in-depth analyses of racial justice struggles and strategies in teacher education. By bringing together counternarratives of critical teacher educators, the editors of this volume present key insights from both individual and collective experiences of advancing racial justice. Written for teacher educators, higher education administrators, policy makers, and others concerned with issues of race, the book is comprised of four parts that each represent a distinct perspective on the struggle for racial justice: contributors reflect on their experiences working as educators of Color to transform the culture of predominately White institutions, navigating the challenges of whiteness within teacher education, building transformational bridges within classrooms, and training current and inservice teachers through concrete models of racial justice. By bringing together these often individualized experiences, *Confronting Racism in Teacher Education* reveals larger patterns that emerge of institutional racism in teacher education, and the strategies that can inspire resistance.

Bree Picower is an Associate Professor in the College of Education and Human Development at Montclair State University.

Rita Kohli is an Assistant Professor in the Education, Society, and Culture Program in the Graduate School of Education at the University of California, Riverside.

Confronting Racism in Teacher Education

Counternarratives of Critical Practice

Edited by Bree Picower and Rita Kohli

Routledge
Taylor & Francis Group

NEW YORK AND LONDON

First published 2017
by Routledge
711 Third Avenue, New York, NY 10017

and by Routledge
2 Park Square, Milton Park, Abingdon, Oxon, OX14 4RN

Routledge is an imprint of the Taylor & Francis Group, an informa business

Library of Congress Cataloging in Publication Data
A catalog record has been requested

ISBN: 978-1-138-65384-9 (hbk)
ISBN: 978-1-138-65385-6 (pbk)
ISBN: 978-1-315-62356-6 (ebk)

Typeset in Bembo
by Saxon Graphics Ltd, Derby

Dedicated to:

Ahmed Mohamed, a 14-year-old Muslim boy who was arrested in school for his science project when teachers accused him of making a bomb (Texas);

A. J. Brooks, a 7-year-old African American girl labeled with a disability who was put in a cage by her teacher (California);

Janissa Valdez, a 6th grade Latina who was body slammed by a school police officer (Texas);

Salecia Johnson, a 6-year-old African American girl handcuffed by police in school for having a "tantrum" (Georgia);

Shakara (identified by first name only), a Black 9th grade girl who was assaulted in class by a school police officer (North Carolina);

Yefri Sorto-Hernandez, a Salvadoran 18-year-old who was picked up by Immigration and Customs Enforcement while waiting at the school bus stop (North Carolina);

Asian American students (California), and Black and Latinx students (Wisconsin, Indiana, Iowa) who were yelled at with racial slurs during school sporting events;

All youth of Color who endure racial violence in schools because they deserve an education that celebrates them, and teachers who fight alongside them for justice.

Contents

Acknowledgments

The editors are extraordinarily grateful and inspired by the book's chapter authors who shared their stories with us and, now, the broader world. It is your willingness to allow yourself to be vulnerable, real, and raw that brought this volume to life and illuminated the themes upon which we can learn and act. We would like to acknowledge our academic family that we are grateful to be a part of. Together we learn, laugh, push, critique, and celebrate as we work collectively in the beautiful struggle. We would also like to thank the following individuals for their assistance in the production of this book: Arturo Nevárez, Simone Goldenstein, William Waters, Grace Ahn and Catherine Bernard.

Bree's acknowledgments: I would like to acknowledge my family, both blood and chosen, who continue to support me. I am grateful for the late night and early morning calls, writing sessions, and reciprocal problem solving we engage in to continue to develop our analysis and work. Love, trust, and vulnerability are part of growing and I thank you for including and engaging with me in the process.

Rita's acknowledgments: I would like to recognize the shoulders I stand upon: my ancestors, grandparents, and especially my parents – Jogindra Prasad Kohli and Neena Mehta Kohli – who retained our language, culture, and ways of being through colonial rule and across continents. It is through you that I know how to live resiliently and with love for my community and identity. I want to acknowledge my partner John who stands in this struggle for justice with me, and our beautiful daughters Asha Devi and Anaya Shanti, whose bright joy for life and learning compel me to work to ensure schools are a place they can find inspiration.

Acknowledgments

1   Introduction

Bree Picower and Rita Kohli

We have been friends and colleagues for years. Having taught in the same school district, lived in several of the same cities, and worked as teacher educators committed to racial justice in urban public schools, we share many experiences, ideologies, and the same community. Simultaneously, our identities have also positioned our entry to this work differently: Bree – a White Jewish New Yorker with a commitment to antiracist work and teacher organizing – has often facilitated the racial analysis development of White teachers, and Rita – a second generation South Asian immigrant, local to California – has focused much of her work on the development and retention of racial justice oriented teachers of Color. These similarities and differences in our professional lives as teacher educators have kept us close as we attempt to navigate, challenge, and transform systemic oppression through our grassroots work with teachers and our respective programs.

One day, several years ago, we were talking on the phone. Bree had been at her institution for several years. Rita was in her second year in a tenure track job and had just come off of maternity leave to the duties of teaching *the* "diversity" class. We enter toward the end of the call:[1]

RITA: Do you have a few more minutes? I'd love to talk something through about work with you.

BREE: Sure, what's up?

RITA: I'm teaching a class in a new program in our college that is not social justice focused at all. It's their last semester before becoming teachers, and the students came to me without much of a structural or racial analysis of schools. I know some students are interested and connected to the material, particularly the students of Color, but there are others who are treating my class like a last hurdle for their degree. I'm struggling in particular with two White male students who are good friends. One of the students responds to me sarcastically in class and last week he yelled at me because he didn't like his grade on a paper. The other student tried to watch a basketball game on his laptop in the middle of another student's facilitation – with the sound ON!!!! They are so resistant to critical content and they are co-opting the class.

BREE: That's outrageous! I'm so sorry that's happening. Their behavior is really crossing a line. I wonder if they would try and get away with that with a White professor? Have you tried getting institutional support?

RITA: I know! Can you imagine? They are going to be someone's teacher in just a few months... I do feel it's racialized and gendered, but I also don't know how to intervene. When I brought it up to my chair she told me there was nothing she could do. We're reminded a lot that we are down on enrollment and need to keep our students happy. In our last faculty meeting, students were actually referred to as "clients," like we're a business that sells teaching degrees to anyone that will buy. I feel so unsupported in holding high and critical expectations for prospective teachers.

BREE: Teacher education is a cash cow for so many universities. Since enrollment is dropping, there is a lot of pressure on us to accept everyone who applies, even if they don't necessarily represent the kind of social justice educator we say we are looking for. It's so frustrating when my students' incoming beliefs are so far from where they need to be as future educators of children of Color. They do grow some, but we have such little time with them before they graduate – it just kills me that some of them are going to be in classrooms with real children, potentially my friends' children, when they have so much further to go.

RITA: I think about that all the time, especially now that I'm a mom. If teacher candidates are our clients, who are K-12 students in that logic? Who are *my* children in that logic? It feels like Black and Brown children are just afterthoughts.

BREE: Exactly.

RITA: I didn't know you struggled with these issues too; it's so helpful to know that this isn't just me – that I'm not just alone in experiencing this.

BREE: I don't think it's exactly the same degree given that I'm White and you're a woman of Color, but I do think all of us doing this race work in teacher ed. are going through it in some way.

This conversation continued as we shared strategies and ideas on how we engage in racial justice work in our programs. As we learned from one another, we felt less isolated. Some of that discourse showed the different ways we approach the work from our varying positionalities. A large part of our discussion also helped to illuminate systematic and persistent racism (including neoliberal racism) that is upheld in teacher education. It became clear to us that change is not possible when we individualize our stories; instead transformation rests upon our collective and institutional analyses of racial justice struggles and strategies in teacher education. In this book, we aim to do just that. By bringing together counternarratives of critical teacher educators we want readers to hear, connect to, and learn from the nuances of individual experiences in the struggle for racial justice in teacher education, but also to see the broader institutional analysis that comes from a collective read of racialized systemic patterns.

Permanence of Racism

Race is a social construct that changes over time. Although it is often (mis)understood as just marking difference, Omi and Winant (1994) defined race as, "an unstable and 'decentered' complex of social meanings constantly being transformed by political struggle" (p. 55). For example, during the era of Americanization schools where Mexican Americans were forcibly sent to shed their language and culture, the label "Mexican" appeared on the 1930 census as a racial category for the first time. On the last census in 2010, the term Mexican only appeared as a specific ethnic marker collapsed under Hispanic (U.S. Census Bureau, 2016), signifying how racial categories are socially constructed and politically driven.

Race is most often used to create or sustain hierarchies of power and dominance, and has consistently been used to include and exclude certain groups from equal participation, resources, and human rights. Thus, it is impossible to disentangle race and racism – a structure of dominance built upon essentialist categories of race (Omi & Winant, 1994). As Fredrick Douglass spoke about racism in 1881,

> In nearly every department of American life [Black Americans] are confronted by this insidious influence. It fills the air. It meets them at the workshop and factory, when they apply for work. It meets them at the church, at the hotel, at the ballot-box, and worst of all, it meets them in the jury-box ... [the Black American] has ceased to be a *slave of an individual*, but has in some sense become *the slave of society*.
> (Douglass in Feagin, 2014, p. 9)

Describing both the permanent and shifting natures of racism in the U.S., Douglass articulated racism as systemic.

Over a century later, scholars of critical race theory purported that racism is a permanent fixture in U.S. institutions. Legal scholar Cheryl Harris (1993) argued that our nation's laws were constructed to protect White property interests starting with the seizure of indigenous land and the appropriation of the bodies and labor of enslaved people. Thus, embedded in our current laws and institutions is an inherent protection of assets associated with whiteness. Harris contended that Whites have a stake in upholding whiteness because it maintains the current social order which has actual material benefits, "Whiteness is an aspect of racial identity surely, but it is much more; it remains a concept based on relations of power, a social construct predicated on white dominance and Black subordination" (p. 1,761). As she pointed out, antiblackness is a tool used to uphold whiteness and White supremacy, and this oppressive racial practice shapes U.S. life and the racism that all people of Color experience.

From the recent lack of indictments of police officers who have killed unarmed Black civilians in cities across the nation to the hate crime murders of churchgoers in Charleston, South Carolina, we see the persistence of antiblackness and racial violence in our current society. Organizing efforts by movements such as Black Lives Matter are heightening public awareness of this racism and calling for a challenge to systems of oppression, yet things have far to shift institutionally.

As a U.S. institution, schools serve to uphold whiteness (Dumas, 2016; Ladson-Billings & Tate, 1995). Ladson-Billings and Tate (1995) argued that schools are designed to serve White interests through disparate resources and opportunities. From the *de jure* segregation of the past to *de facto* segregation today, inequalities in school funding have consistently provided students of Color overcrowded, underresourced educational opportunities compared to their White peers (Oakes, Rogers, & Silver, 2004; Anyon, 2005). From threats of lynching during integration (Beals, 1995), to school police, pushout, and criminalization in schools today (Kim, Losen, & Hewitt, 2010), students of Color have consistently received a message of inferiority and marginalization within schools. Standard curriculum and traditional pedagogy have been equally noted to lack the history, perspectives, and values of minoritized communities throughout the trajectory of U.S. schools (Woodson, 1933; Loewen, 2008).

Confronted with racism in education, there is also a tradition of resistance (Solórzano & Delgado Bernal, 2002), where critical individuals and collectives have always pushed for change. Key education scholars have built upon critical race frameworks to deconstruct the ways that schools, fraught with institutionalized racism, affirm the racial status quo (Ladson-Billings & Tate, 1995; Solórzano, 1997; Solórzano, Ceja, & Yosso, 2000; Parker & Lynn, 2002; Dixson & Rousseau, 2006). These and other race scholars have illuminated how institutional culpability is often masked by ideologies, policies, and practices of deficit thinking (Valencia & Solórzano, 1997; Valencia, 2012); the ignoring of race or racial difference (Bonilla-Silva, 2010),[2] and meritocracy – the belief that success is always the product of individual merit (Au, 2015), leaving racism in schools untouched but often invisibilized. Students, community members, and teachers have organized, marched, and posed demands for decades in the name of educational equity and racial justice (Briscoe & Khalifa, 2015; Berta-Ávila, Revilla, & Figueroa, 2011; Solórzano & Delgado Bernal, 2002; Stovall, 2013), as well as collectivized against injustices such as the school to prison pipeline (Ayers, Dohrn, & Ayers, 2001), privatization (Fabricant & Fine, 2013; Lipman, 2011), and high-stakes testing (Au, 2010; 2015).

This book aims to understand the ways in which critical teacher educators experience, confront, and resist racism in teacher education. By collectivizing often individualized experiences, larger patterns emerge of how teacher education as an institution contributes to the permanence of racism, as well as strategies of resistance that can inspire and embolden other teacher educators working to confront racism in their settings.

Context of Teacher Education

Teacher education does not exist in a vacuum; rather it reflects and perpetuates the system of White supremacy and economic inequity written about above. Teacher education is not immune to the rapidly changing forces of privatization advancing on K-12 education; in fact there has been a proliferation of external, top-down school reform efforts in K-12 public education (Kumashiro, 2012; Lipman, 2011; Ravitch, 2013). External evaluations such as those of the National Council of Teacher Quality, standards such as those of the Council for the Accreditation of Educator Preparation, and outside accountability measures such as Education Teacher Performance Assessment (edTPA) are a major part of the rapidly shifting landscape of teacher education (Dover & Schultz, 2016; Picower & Marshall, in press).

These neoliberal reforms both advance the current economic and racial order (Picower & Mayorga, 2015) while simultaneously creating barriers for the role that teacher education can play in advancing racial justice. For instance, under No Child Left Behind, teacher quality was narrowly defined (Cochran-Smith et al., 2009; Sleeter, 2008) in ways that removed a mandate on education schools to prepare candidates around root causes of inequity (Landorf & Nevin, 2007). In fact, in 2006, NCATE, the nation's largest organization accrediting teacher education programs removed social justice from its standards used to evaluate teacher education programs (Wilson, 2007). Such reforms put pressure on schools of education to move away from issues of race while the increased focus on methods or content areas aligned with K-12 testing often results in the removal of courses or institutional focus on areas such as social or racial justice that do not fall into a tested content area (Sleeter, 2008). Additionally, online and alternative preparation programs have put pressure on university programs to significantly cut their credit hours, ensuring that diversity topic areas that do not fall neatly into academic disciplines are the first to go (Sleeter, 2008). All of these trends create barriers to advancing racial justice within teacher education.

Simultaneous to this encroachment of market based reforms that reinforce and maintain racial and economic inequality, there is a cultural disconnect between increasingly diverse student populations in public schools and the overwhelmingly White and middle class teaching force (Boser, 2011; Easton-Brooks, 2015). Thus, concurrent to teaching content and methods, teacher education programs must also equip teachers with racial, cultural, and structural analyses of schooling (Cochran-Smith, 2004). To effectively respond to their students and families, K-12 educators must enter schools prepared to recognize, name, and address issues of racial injustice that exist within and outside the walls of schools (Ladson-Billings, 2001; Sleeter, 2001). There is a growing body of scholarship that identifies the importance of these learning dimensions, and argues for a focus on racial justice within teacher education (Ayers, Quinn, & Stovall, 2008; Gorski, Zenkov, Osei-Kofi & Sapp, 2012; Kumashiro, 2015). Research in this area has often focused on two main topics: 1) preparing teachers to understand the role of race and racism in the experiences of students and communities; and 2) unpacking teacher racial identities as they connect to classroom pedagogy.

Many studies have argued the need for teacher candidates to understand students' racial and cultural identity, and the intersection this has with schooling experiences (Nieto & Bode, 2011; Howard, 2001; Tatum, 1999). Other studies argue that teachers must be prepared to address racial inequity in student achievement (Boykin & Noguera, 2011; Ladson-Billings, 2006). There is also a research focus on the racial identity of teacher candidates and how race shapes their ideology, including studies focused on White teachers working with students of Color (Picower, 2012; Howard, 1999), issues of cultural match (Sleeter, 2001; Achinstein & Ogawa, 2011; Delpit, 2006), and a growing focus on teachers of Color (Amos, 2010; Dixson & Dingus, 2008; Kohli, 2009; Villegas & Jordan Irvine, 2010). Additionally, a large body of literature emphasizes the need for multicultural (Banks, 1999; Grant & Sleeter, 2008) or culturally relevant pedagogy, as it has been demonstrated to have positive impacts on students of Color (Ladson-Billings, 1994; Villegas & Lucas, 2002).

While this research has called for attention to race and racism in teacher education, advancing racial justice in this field is not easily accomplished. The neoliberal reforms mentioned above that welcomed externally mandated course requirements and high-stakes testing into teacher education have narrowed the curriculum and resulted in a de-professionalization of teacher educators (Kumashiro, 2012; Sleeter, 2008; Ravitch, 2013; Gorlewski, 2013; Picower & Marshall, in press). Those committed to challenging the status quo and using education as a vehicle for change are pushing back against these structures, but the current context makes the already difficult work of addressing racial inequities through the academy even more daunting.

Adding to the difficulty is the enduring presence of institutional racism and the culture of whiteness within the academy. Research has uncovered the hostile racial climates that faculty and staff of Color endure within higher education (Hurtado, Milem, Clayton-Pedersen, & Allen, 1999; Jayakumar, Howard, Allen, & Han, 2009), particularly those who challenge the status quo (Gutiérrez y Muhs, Niemann, González, & Harris, 2012). While more recent statistics have been difficult to uncover, as of ten years ago, 88% of the teacher education force was White and the climate was racially hostile, reflective of broader university contexts (Ladson-Billings, 2005). This was in part due to the racial demographics, but it has also been noted that the ideological beliefs of many teacher educators contribute to the status quo

(Kea, Campbell-Whatley, & Richards, 2006). On a more structural level, Cross (2005) in her conceptualization of the "new racism of teacher education" exposes how in teacher education programs, "White privilege is maintained through invisible, insidious operations of power that foster whiteness and racism. This power is no longer enacted primarily through physical violence but is mostly achieved through more symbolic power" (p. 267). Kea, Trent, and Davis (2002) argue that there is a lack of willingness or capacity to integrate issues of race in a coherent way throughout teacher education programs. Thus, instead of preparing the racial literacy of teachers (Skerrett, 2011), teacher education is fraught with "soft approaches to multiculturalism, diversity and urban education; resistance by students and even some teacher educators to such discussions; and the ignoring of issues of racism, power, and whiteness" (p. 266).

Despite the challenges, many within the field of teacher education take a critical approach to their work and are committed to advancing racial justice. Just as racism takes many forms, so does the resistance to it within teacher education. While there are many working to reform educational policy (Lipman, 2011), this book includes various examples of teacher educators who are confronting and addressing day-to-day manifestations on structural and interpersonal levels. For some, it means creating strategies, courses, and programs that work to transform the racial analysis of future teachers (see Sealey-Ruiz, Chapter 16; de los Ríos & Souto-Manning, Chapter 19, all this volume); or creating pipeline programs to recruit (see Camangian, Chapter 3, this volume) or maintain teachers of Color in the profession (see Curammeng & Tintiangco-Cubales, Chapter 21; Pizarro, Chapter 20, both this volume). For others, the resistance is focused on critiquing and organizing against market based reforms such as edTPA (see Dover, Chapter 6, this volume). Just as collective movements are working toward educational justice in the K–12 arena, teacher educators are fighting back through a myriad of critical practices.

This book focuses on the issues that arise as such critical teacher educators work to advance racial justice. Although there are many lessons to be learned from these teacher educators, very little scholarship focuses on such issues (Marx, 2006; Villegas & Lucas, 2002; Zeichner, 2009). In addition, this limited scholarship tends to overlook the positionality of teacher educators and instead frames them as a monolithic group. Much like the raced, classed, and gendered identities of students and teachers, the identity of a teacher educator also inevitably anchors and shapes their approaches to racial justice. To build on this reality, this book moves away from evasive approaches to race or racial differences of teacher educators to a more complex analysis of how their positionality impacts both their experiences and their racial justice pedagogies.

Methods

As mentioned at the beginning of this chapter, we (Bree and Rita) have always openly discussed the challenges and opportunities afforded each of us given our different positionalities in our teaching about race. As teacher educators who engage in teaching and organizing around issues of race, we have listened, learned, consoled, commiserated, and celebrated our different experiences over the course of our decade of friendship and working toward racial justice in teacher education. We understand that the work looks different for us both given our individual racial identities and have spent hours teasing those differences apart. While these were conversations that we had together and with other teacher educators of multiple intersectional identities in the hallways of conferences or in private moments, we felt that understanding teacher educator identities in the pursuit of racial justice is needed to continue to move the work forward. Rather than take a one-size-fits-all approach to the positionality of teacher educators, we want to better understand how those who work to advance racial justice through teacher education do so while confronting racism and navigating their own intersectional identities.

We felt this was an area ripe for broader exploration. Our hunch was proved correct when we received over 120 responses to our call for chapter proposals for teacher educators to center their voice and experiences as they confront racism in or through teacher education. Clearly we had struck a chord. After carefully culling the proposals, we (somewhat painfully) narrowed it down to a select group of critical teacher educators of non-dominant positionalities (meaning that prominent aspects of their identities do not carry majority status and/or power). We chose chapters from scholars who expressed systemic analyses of racism and other forms of oppression, applied theory to frame and reframe experiences with power, and engaged in asset framings of communities of Color. Their narratives spoke to the range of challenges experienced and strategies used while working toward racial justice. We purposefully selected participants who were diverse in terms of race/ethnicity, gender, sexual orientation, religion, their position within teacher education (i.e. tenure track, clinical, adjunct), how long they had been in the field, and the geographic region in which they worked.

This book is a collective of counternarratives – 16 stories from non-dominant, self-identified critical teacher educators speaking back from the margins, as well as six case studies of innovations that extend the borders of teacher education to develop teachers' racial analysis, and illuminate potentiality within teacher education. In contrast to a *dominant narrative,* which is a story or perspective that comes from the vantage point of the powerful, commonly accepted as truth, a counternarrative is told from the vantage point of those oppressed and is a means to challenge power. It is a story that reveals structures and practices that contribute to inequality and challenge deficit myths (Yosso, 2005). Milner and Howard (2013) argue that counternarratives can be used as a tool of analysis "to complement, nuance, disrupt and counter storylines in teacher education" that maintain the dominant perspective as race is consistently overlooked or undertheorized in this field. They maintain that "A counter-narrative provides space for researchers to reinterpret, disrupt or to interrupt pervasive discourses." As such, they continue, "These narratives represent non-mainstream stories which represent other truths, and other experiences that directly refute hegemony" (p. 542).

Counternarratives have a rich tradition in education scholarship. In critical race theory, counternarratives (also called counterstories) have been used by communities of Color to challenge majoritarian stories of power (Perez Huber, 2008; Solórzano & Yosso, 2001; Yosso, 2006). Starting with Derrick Bell's *Faces at the Bottom of the Well: The Permanence of Racism* (1992) and Richard Delgado's *The Rodrigo Chronicles* (1995) counternarratives have served to reframe and rewrite deficit stories of people of Color that have traditionally been accepted as truth (Solórzano & Yosso, 2001). As Milner and Howard assert, "the counter-narrative allows the researcher and participants to study and name a reality inconsistent with what might be considered the norm or pervasive otherwise" (Ladson-Billings, 1998, p. 542).

Because of our focus on understanding racism within teacher education, to build upon the experiential knowledge and perspectives of those racially marginalized, we ensured that the majority of our contributors were teacher educators of Color. And while the tradition of counternarratives often focuses on the voices of people of Color, we chose to also include the narratives of three White teacher educators who represent intersectional non-dominant positions and are speaking back to whiteness because we felt their analysis added a complexity to our structural understanding of racial injustice. In the field of DisCrit, which examines the intersections of race and "dis/abilities," Connor, Ferri, & Annamma (2016) rely on Gilbourn's assertion that,

> it is fine for a primary interest to drive a researcher, but imperative that other dimensions must be taken seriously within the work... Thus, by analyzing multiple dimensions within a specific context, researchers are able to see how they can mesh, blur, overlap and interact in various ways to reveal knowledge.
>
> (p. 12)

Including intersecting oppressions in our analysis, we hoped to see how whiteness shapeshifts within teacher education for diverse people with shared goals of racial justice. This informed our selection process as we made sure we included teacher educators who self-identified in a variety of ways: people of Color who identified from a variety of racial and ethnic groups (e.g., African American, biracial, Asian American, Latinx), teacher educators who identified as male, female, and trans; queer, bisexual, and straight teacher educators, people with (dis)abilities. As Collins states "the notion of intersectionality describes microlevel processes – namely, how each individual and group occupies a social position within interlocking structures of oppression described by the metaphor of intersectionality. Together they shape oppression" (Collins in Connor et al., 2016, p. 15). The counternarratives selected explore these microlevel processes that individual teacher educators experienced, but collectively reveal the patterns of oppression within teacher education and how the field contributes to the maintenance of White supremacy.

It is not just the narrative that is important to tell, there is also a significance in how we hear and treat non-dominant stories. Cruz (2012) puts forth that testimonio (a form of narrative methodology that emerged from Latinx scholars):

> demands rapt listening and its inherent intersubjectivity when we have learned to do the kind of radical listening demanded by a testimonialist, turning all of us who are willing to participate as listener, storyteller, or researcher into witnesses whether we come from a place of political solidarity or even from places of conflict.   →indigisures

We echo this call for solidarity and invite the reader to take seriously the collective themes of racism these stories provide. Whether the reader sees themselves in the experiences or are able to develop empathy with the storytellers, the responsibility lies with us to build and act upon the themes as we confront racism within our own settings.

What We Learned

When we wrote the call for proposals, we thought the significant theme of the book would be how teacher educators of multiple intersectional identities maneuver to advance racial justice in their work. However, upon reading the proposals, the throughline that powerfully emerged were stories of incredible trauma, as well as resistance and resilience, that teacher educators face in working toward racial justice. In attempting to address issues of race in settings steeped in institutional racism, with colleagues and students who resist attempts at challenging their hegemonic ideologies of whiteness, the teacher educators expressed feelings of isolation, alienation, inadequacy, shame, and guilt. Because of the isolated ways in which they engage in this work, often apparently as the only ones committed to ideals of racial justice in our institutions, the teacher educators' stories tended to individualize the stress and pain of these seemingly private stories they felt they were battling alone.

What was revealed to us as editors with the opportunity to carefully read each of the narratives was that these are not just personal stories – rather they are patterns of how institutional racism operates to maintain the permanence of racism. By looking across the counternarratives, we saw how racism individualizes our work, divides and conquers, leading those of us committed to racial justice to internalize the associated shame and guilt of the impossible task of defeating racism on our own. It also showed the strength and power that critical teacher educators have to challenge racism and shift the institutional culture. Chapter authors revealed that writing these stories felt cathartic because putting their struggles into theoretically framed chapters helped transform what they felt as a vulnerable experience into an act of collective resistance by calling out institutionalized racism. The aim of this book is to provide the reader this same opportunity to understand how each of these stories exists within larger patterns of how racism is maintained and to situate themselves within this context. These stories provide us with ways to not only identify with, or learn from, others with similar aims, but to also identify our seemingly personal challenges as part of a larger collective of resistance struggles in the face of institutional racism. By understanding the patterns of racism, we also hope to illuminate the potential for paths of collective resistance.

Book Structure

The book is divided into four parts: 1) Paving the Way; 2) Navigating Whiteness; 3) Building for Transformation; and 4) Pushing the Borders of Teacher Education. These parts represent the different ways that the included authors describe their work to advance racial justice in teacher education.

Part I: Paving the Way

The first part includes four chapters from teacher educators (Sonia Nieto; Patrick Roz Camangian; Tyrone Howard; and Mari Ann Banks (Roberts)) who have created paths for people of Color within a White-dominated professional context. These authors have "paved the way" by serving as the sole educator of Color (often intersectional with other forms of marginalization) within their institutions, fearlessly creating new pipelines to diversity within both the teaching force and teacher education, standing as role models and mentors for those who follow, and gracefully drawing a line for what is no longer tolerable within a context of neoliberal reform. This part highlights the importance of powerful individuals who build upon their positionality to challenge and transform the demographics and culture of teacher education.

Part II: Navigating Whiteness

This includes five counternarratives (Alison G. Dover; Daren Graves; Jillian Carter Ford; Alana D. Murry & Heather E. Yuhaniak; and Noemí Cortés) of teacher educators representing diverse positionalities who are negotiating the challenges of whiteness within teacher education. From dealing with the impact of external mandates that negatively impact racial justice work, to working with resistant students, to being positioned problematically by colleagues, to addressing White fragility, and making a stand within their institutions; these chapters highlight the toll such work presents on the emotional and professional experiences of racial justice oriented teacher educators. Based on their identities, they navigate these experiences differently and these nuances provide a broader understanding of what it looks like to work toward racial justice from multiple vantage points.

Part III: Building for Transformation

The third part includes five chapters by teacher educators (Tanya Maloney; Harper Benjamin Keenan; Joanne Tien; Sameena Eidoo; and Eduardo Lara) who have used their positionalities to build bridges as a means to challenge racial injustice. From bringing one's whole self to the classroom, to developing allies and solidarity with students, to questioning who is privileged within democratic pedagogy, to building on teachable moments; each of these chapters emphasizes the significance of positionality in relationality and transformation.

Part IV: Pushing the Borders of Teacher Education

The final part of the book includes six shorter cases by teachers, teacher educators, and educational activists (Yolanda Sealey-Ruiz; LaToya Strong, Margrit Pittman-Polletta, & Daralee Vázquez-García; Antonio Nieves Martinez; Cati de los Ríos & Mariana Souto-Manning; Marcos Pizarro; Edward R. Curammeng & Allyson Tintiangco-Cubales) that describe successful models of addressing racial justice in the preparation or continuing education of teachers. Ranging from full programs to smaller initiatives, the creators of these projects provide concrete models of racial justice outside of the traditional boundaries of teacher preparation. The examples in this part, embedded in the context of the broader book, provide a range of potential directions for readers to consider as they reframe or reimagine possibilities within teacher education.

Notes

1 This is a reconstructed dialogue based on our collective memory of a phone conversation we had in Spring 2013.
2 Bonilla-Silva (2010) described this process as "colorblindness," yet critical disability scholars have complicated the term, critiquing the way it "likens a lack of vision to ignorance" (Annamma, Connor, & Ferri, 2013) and recommend a shift to Frankenberg's (1993) and Stubblefield's (2005) use of the term "color-evasiveness" which "refuses to position people who are blind as embodying deficit" (p. 6). Thus while we find meaning in Bonilla-Silva's definition of the concept, and Annamma et al.'s critique, we have chosen to avoid the use of either term because we do not believe in the use of "color" as a proxy for race.

References

Achinstein, B., & Ogawa, R. (2011). *Change(d) Agents: New teachers of Color in urban Schools*. New York, NY: Teachers College Press.

Amos, Y. T. (2010). "They don't want to get it!" Interaction between minority and white pre-service teachers in a multicultural education class., *Multicultural Education, 17*(4), 31–37.

Annamma, S. A., Connor, D., & Ferri, B. (2013). Dis/ability critical race studies (DisCrit): Theorizing at the intersections of race and dis/ability. *Race Ethnicity and Education, 16*(1), 1–31.

Anyon, J. (2005). *Radical Possibilities: Public policy, urban education, and a new social movement*. New York, NY: Routledge.

Au, W. (2010). *Unequal by Design: High-stakes testing and the standardization of inequality*. Abingdon, UK: Routledge.

Au, W. (2015). Meritocracy 2.0 high-stakes, Standardized testing as a racial project of neoliberal multiculturalism. *Educational Policy, 30*(1), 39–62. DOI: 10.1177/0895904815614916.

Ayers, W., Dohrn, B., & Ayers, R. (2001). *Zero Tolerance: Resisting the drive for punishment in our schools: A handbook for parents, students, educators, and citizens*. New York, NY: New Press.

Ayers, W., Quinn, T., & Stovall, D. (Eds.). (2008). *Handbook of Social Justice in Education*. New York, NY: Routledge.

Banks, J. A. (1999). *An Introduction to Multicultural Education* (2nd ed.). Boston, MA: Allyn and Bacon.

Beals, M. (1995). *Warriors Don't Cry: Searing memoir of battle to integrate Little Rock*. New York, NY: Simon and Schuster.

Bell, D. A. (1992). *Faces at the Bottom of the Well: The permanence of racism*. New York, NY: Basic Books.

Berta-Ávila, M., Revilla, A. T., & Figueroa, J. L. (2011). *Marching Students: Chicana and Chicano activism in education, 1968 to the present*. Reno, NV: University of Nevada Press.

Bonilla-Silva, E. (2010). *Racism Without Racists: Color-blind racism and the persistence of racial inequality in the United States*. New York, NY: Rowman & Littlefield [new chapter on the Obama phenomenon].

Boser, U. (2011). Teacher diversity matters: A state by state analysis of teachers of Color. *Report for the Center for American Progress*. Washington, DC: Center for American Progress.

Boykin, A. W., & Noguera, P. (2011). *Creating the Opportunity to Learn: Moving from research to practice to close the achievement gap*. Alexandria, VA: ASCD.

Briscoe, F. M., & Khalifa, M. A. (2015). "That racism thing": A critical race discourse analysis of a conflict over the proposed closure of a black high school. *Race Ethnicity and Education, 18*(6), 739–763.

Cochran-Smith, M. (2004). *Walking the Road: Race, diversity, and social justice in teacher education*. New York, NY: Teachers College Press.

Cochran-Smith, M., Shakman, K., Jong, C., Terrell, D., Barnatt, J., & McQuillah, P. (2009). Good and just teaching: The case for social justice in teacher education. *American Journal of Education, 115*(3), 347–377.

Connor, D., Ferri, B., & Annamma, S. (2016). *DisCrit: Disability studies and critical race theory in education*. New York, NY: Teacher's College Press.

Cross, B. E. (2005). New racism, reformed teacher education, and the same ole' oppression. *Educational Studies, 38*(3), 263–274.

Cruz, C. (2012). Making curriculum from scratch: Testimonio in an urban classroom. *Equity & Excellence in Education, 45*(3), 460–471.

Delgado, R. (1995). *The Rodrigo Chronicles. Conversations about race and America.* New York, NY: New York University Press.

Delpit, L. D. (2006). *Other People's Children: Cultural conflict in the classroom.* New York, NY: The New Press.

Dixson, A., & Dingus, J. (2008). In search of our mothers' gardens: Black women teachers and professional socialization. *Teachers College Record, 110*(4), 805–837.

Dixson, A., & Rousseau, C. K. (2006). *Critical Race Theory in Education: All God's children got a song.* New York, NY: Taylor & Francis.

Dover, A. G., & Schultz, B. D. (2016, January). Troubling the edTPA: Illusions of objectivity and rigor. *The Educational Forum 80*(1), 95–106. Routledge.

Dumas, M. J. (2016). "Be real Black for me." Imagining BlackCrit in education. *Urban Education, 51*(3), 343–360. 0042085916628611.

Easton-Brooks, D. (2015). Bridging the gap and diversifying teaching education. *The Race Controversy in American Education [2 volumes],* 259. Westport, CT: Praeger Publishing.

Fabricant, M., & Fine, M. (2013). *The Changing Politics of Education: Privatization and the dispossessed lives left behind.* Boulder, CO: Paradigm Publishers

Feagin, J. R. (2014). *Racist America: Roots, current realities, and future reparations.* New York, NY: Routledge.

Frankenberg, R. (1993). *White Women, Race Matters.* Minneapolis, MN: University of Minnesota Press.

Gorlewski, J. (2013). In D. Ravitch (Ed.), *What Is edTPA and Why Do Critics Dislike It?* Retrieved from http://dianeravitch.net/2013/06/03/what-is-edtpa-and-why-do-critics-dislike-it/

Gorski, P., Zenkov, K., Osei-Kofi, N., & Sapp, J. (2012). *Cultivating Social Justice Teachers.* Sterling, VA: Stylus Publishing, LLC.

Grant, C. A., & Sleeter, C. E. (2008). *Turning on Learning: Five approaches for multicultural teaching plans for race, class, gender, and disability.* (5th ed.) Columbus, OH: Merrill.

Gutiérrez y Muhs, G., Niemann, Y. F., González, C. G., & Harris, A. P. (Eds.). (2012). *Presumed Incompetent: The intersections of race and class for women in academia.* Boulder, CO: University Press of Colorado.

Harris, C. I. (1993). Whiteness as property. *Harvard Law Review 106*(8), 1710–1712.

Howard, G. R. (1999). *We Can't Teach What We Don't Know: White teachers, multiracial schools.* New York, NY: Teachers College Press.

Howard, T. C. (2001). Telling their side of the story: African-American students' perceptions of culturally relevant teaching. *The Urban Review, 33*(2), 131–149.

Hurtado, S., Milem, J., Clayton-Pedersen, A., & Allen, W. (1999). Enacting diverse learning environments: Improving the climate for racial/ethnic diversity in higher education. *ASHE-ERIC Higher Education Report 26*(8).

Jayakumar, U., Howard, T., Allen, W., & Han, J. (2009). Racial privilege in the professoriate: An exploration of campus racial climate, retention and satisfaction. *Journal of Higher Education, 80*(5), 538–563.

Kea, C., Campbell-Whatley, G. D., & Richards, H. V. (2006). *Becoming Culturally Responsive Educators: Rethinking teacher education pedagogy.* Tempe, AZ: NCCREST

Kea, C., Trent, S. C., & Davis, C. P. (2002). African American student teachers' perceptions about preparedness to teach students from culturally and linguistically diverse backgrounds. *Multiple Perspectives, 4*(1), 18–25.

Kim, C. Y., Losen, D. J., & Hewitt, D. T. (2010). *The School-to-Prison Pipeline: Structuring legal reform.* New York, NY: New York University Press.

Kohli, R. (2009). Critical race reflections: Valuing the experiences of teachers of color in teacher education. *Race Ethnicity and Education, 12*(2), 235–251.

Kumashiro, K. (2012). *Bad Teacher: How blaming teachers distorts the bigger picture.* New York, NY: Teachers College Press.

Kumashiro, K. (2015). *Against Common Sense.* (3rd ed.) New York, NY: Routledge.

Ladson-Billings, G. (1994). *The Dreamkeepers: Successful teachers of African American children* (1st ed.). San Francisco, CA: Jossey-Bass Publishers.

Ladson-Billings, G. (1998). Just what is critical race theory and what's it doing in a nice field like education? *International Journal of Qualitative Studies in Education, 11*(1), 7–24.

Ladson-Billings, G. (2001). *Crossing Over to Canaan: The journey of new teachers in diverse classrooms* (1st ed.). San Francisco, CA: Jossey-Bass Publishers.

Ladson-Billings, G. (2005). The evolving role of critical race theory in educational scholarship. *Race, Ethnicity and Education, 8*(1), 115–119.

Ladson-Billings, G. (2006). From the achievement gap to the education debt: Understanding achievement in US schools. *Educational Researcher, 35*(7), 3–12.

Ladson-Billings, G., & Tate IV, W. F. (1995). Towards a critical race theory of education. *Teachers College Record, 97*(1), 47–68.

Landorf, H., & Nevin, A. (2007). Social justice as a disposition for teacher education programs: Why is it such a problem? In S. M. Nielsen & M. S. Plakhotnik (Eds.), *Proceedings of the Sixth Annual College of Education Research Conference: Urban and international education section* (pp. 49–53). Miami, FL: Florida International University. http://coeweb.fiu.edu/research_conference/

Lipman, P. (2011). *The New Political Economy of Urban Education: Neoliberalism, race, and the right to the city.* New York, NY: Routledge.

Loewen, J. W. (2008). *Lies My Teacher Told Me: Everything your American history textbook got wrong.* New York, NY: New Press.

Marx, S. (2006). *Revealing the Invisible: Confronting passive racism in teacher education.* New York, NY: Routledge.

Milner IV, H. R., & Howard, T. C. (2013). Counter-narrative as method: Race, policy and research for teacher education. *Race Ethnicity and Education, 16*(4), 536–561.

Nieto, S., & Bode, P. (2011). *Affirming Diversity: The sociopolitical context of multicultural education.* New York, NY: Longman.

Oakes, J., Rogers, J., & Silver, D. (2004). *Separate and Unequal 50 Years After Brown: California's racial "opportunity gap".* Report published by UCLA's Institute for Democracy, Education and Access. Los Angeles, CA: UCLA/IDEA.

Omi, M., & Winant, H. (1994). *Racial Formation in the United States: From 1960s to 1990s.* New York, NY: Routledge.

Parker, L., & Lynn, M. (2002). What's race got to do with it? Critical race theory's conflicts with and connections to qualitative research methodology and epistemology. *Qualitative Inquiry, 8*(1), 7–22.

Perez Huber, L. (2008). Building critical race methodologies in educational research: A research note on critical race testimonio. *FIU L. Rev.*, *4*, 159.

Picower, B. (2012). *Practice What You Teach: Social justice education in the classroom and the streets*. New York, NY: Routledge.

Picower, B. & Marshall, A. (2016). "Run like hell" to "look before you leap": Faculty responses to preparing teachers for diversity in the wake of edTPA. In J. Carter & H. Lochte, *Teacher Performance Assessment and Accountability Reforms: The impacts of edTPA on teaching and schools*. New York, NY: Palgrave MacMillan Publishing.

Picower, B. & Mayorga, E. (2015). *What's Race Got To Do With It: How current school reform policy maintains inequality*. Edited book for Peter Lang Publishers' series Critical Multicultural Perspectives on Whiteness. New York, NY: Peter Lang.

Ravitch, D. (2013). *Reign of Error: The hoax of the privatization movement and the danger to America's public schools*. New York, NY: Alfred A. Knopf.

Skerrett, A. (2011). English teachers' racial literacy knowledge and practice. *Race Ethnicity and Education*, *14*(3), 313–330.

Sleeter, C. E. (2001). Preparing teachers for culturally diverse schools: Research and the overwhelming presence of whiteness. *Journal of Teacher Education*, *52*(2), 94–106.

Sleeter, C. E. (2008). Teacher education, neoliberalism, and social justice. In W. C. Ayers, T. Quinn, & D. Stovall (Eds.), *Handbook of Social Justice in Education*. New York, NY: Routledge.

Solórzano, D. G. (1997). Images and words that wound: Critical race theory, racial stereotyping, and teacher education. *Teacher Education Quarterly*, *24*, 5–19.

Solórzano, D. G., & Delgado Bernal, D. (2001). Examining transformational resistance through a critical race and LatCrit theory framework: Chicana and Chicano students in an urban context. *Urban Education*, *36*(3), 308–342.

Solórzano, D., & Yosso, T. J. (2001). From racial stereotyping and deficit discourse toward a critical race theory in teacher education. *Multicultural Education*, *9*(1), 2.

Solórzano, D., Ceja, M., & Yosso, T. (2000). Critical race theory, racial microaggressions, and campus racial climate: The experiences of African American college students. *Journal of Negro Education*, *69*(1–2), 60–73.

Stovall, D. (2013). 14 souls, 19 days and 1600 dreams: Engaging critical race praxis while living on the 'edge' of race. *Discourse: Studies in the Cultural Politics of Education, 34*(4), 562–578.

Stubblefield, A. (2005). *Ethics along the Color Line*. Ithaca, NY: Cornell University Press.

Tatum, B. D. (1999). *"Why Are All the Black Kids Sitting Together in the Cafeteria?" and Other Conversations About Race*. New York, NY: Basic Books.

U.S. Census Bureau. (2016). *Quick Facts from the U.S. Census Bureau*. Retrieved from https://www.census.gov/quickfacts/table/PST045215/00

Valencia, R. R. (Ed.). (2012). *The Evolution of Deficit Thinking: Educational thought and practice*. New York, NY: RoutledgeFalmer.

Valencia, R. R. & Solórzano, D. G. (1997). Contemporary deficit thinking. In R. Valencia (ed.), *The Evolution of Deficit Thinking: Educational thought and practice* (pp. 160–210). New York, NY: RoutledgeFalmer.

Villegas, A., & Jordan Irvine, J. (2010). "Diversifying the teaching force: An examination of major arguments." *Urban Review*, *42*(3): 175–192.

Villegas, A., & Lucas, T. (2002). *Educating Culturally Responsive Teachers: A conceptually coherent and structurally integrated approach*. Albany, NY: SUNY Press.

Wilson, R. (2007). *Teacher-Education Accreditor Formally Drops Social-Justice Language.* Retrieved from http://chronicle.com/article/Teacher-Education-Accreditor/ 39830

Woodson, C. G. (1933). *The Mis-education of the Negro.* Trenton, NJ: Africa World Press.

Yosso, T. J. (2005). Whose culture has capital? A critical race theory discussion of community cultural wealth. *Race Ethnicity and Education, 8*(1), 69–91.

Yosso, T. J. (2006). *Critical Race Counterstories along the Chicana/Chicano Educational Pipeline.* New York, NY: Routledge.

Zeichner, K. M. (2009). *Teacher Education and the Struggle for Social Justice.* New York, NY: Routledge.

Part I
Paving the Way

Spanish Speaking

2   Identity Matters

My Life as a [Puerto Rican] Teacher Educator

Sonia Nieto

I began my teaching career at an intermediate school in Brooklyn, New York in 1966. Two years later, I moved to P.S. 25 in the Bronx, the first public bilingual school in the Northeast. An innovative school, P.S. 25 was based on two important ideas: that bilingualism was an asset upon which teachers and students could build, and that parent involvement was a crucial factor in student success. I was not fully convinced of either of these ideas when I began teaching at that school (after all, I had never had the benefits of a bilingual education myself, and my parents had never been "involved" in the traditional sense of that word), but I became a firm believer of both within a couple of months.

At P.S. 25, everyone was either already bilingual or becoming bilingual, from students to teachers, from the principal to the janitor. It was the first place I worked where being Puerto Rican and speaking Spanish were seen as assets, where I felt affirmed for who I was and what I brought to the job. It was at that school where I learned that identity matters, this in spite of the message I had received in my teacher preparation program to "leave your culture baggage at the door." I remained at that school for four years, first as a fourth-grade teacher and, later, as a curriculum specialist. Those years were to have an indelible impact on my life and my philosophy of teaching.

I brought what I had learned at P.S. 25 to my next position as a faculty member in the Puerto Rican Studies Department at Brooklyn College. It was 1972, the height of the Civil Rights, bilingual education, and ethnic studies movements, and the beginning of the demand for multicultural education in public schools. I was 29 years old.

Baptism by Fire in Academia

The Puerto Rican Studies Department at Brooklyn College, in only its third year of existence, was just starting a bilingual education sequence co-sponsored by the School of Education. As one of the first bilingual teachers in the city, I was recruited for one of the faculty positions. I was thrilled to be there, but as one of a tiny number of Puerto Rican faculty members at the college, I also felt like a fish out of water. So, when I went to my first Faculty Senate meeting after being elected as the departmental representative, I remember looking around and feeling conspicuous. The only Puerto Rican member of that body of mostly White males, I was also the youngest and one of the few women. And because our department was in constant flux due to student and faculty activism and demands, we faculty members from the Department of Puerto Rican Studies seemed even more out of place in an academic setting.

Like ethnic studies, bilingual education too was born of struggle and activism. As a result, those of us in the bilingual component of the department faced a double burden: fighting for bilingual education in K-12 education, and working to legitimize ethnic studies as a credible academic program. Through a combination of chance, family support, a changing sociopolitical context, and opportunities that opened up after we moved from a low income to a middle class neighborhood when I was in junior high school, I was one of the relatively few Puerto Ricans to make it through the New York City public schools. It helped enormously as well that I was a light-skinned Puerto Rican who was (and is still) often presumed to be White, making my introduction to, and acceptance in, academia and other settings far less daunting than for darker-skinned Puerto Ricans.

We were eight faculty members in the Puerto Rican Studies Department, with three of us part of the bilingual education component. Half of us were hired as instructors since we did not have doctorates, a situation to be expected given the tiny number of U.S.-based Puerto Ricans with advanced degrees at the time. As a result, unlike faculty in other departments, most of us had not been apprenticed into academia through a doctoral program by a learned major advisor. We had also not presented our work at conferences nor had we collaborated with senior professors to publish our first articles. No, we had gotten to academia through other means: work in the public schools, activism in the streets, and advocacy through various venues. We were unaccustomed to the work of academia: preparing courses, advising students, holding office hours, doing research, and publishing were all new to us.

Working at Brooklyn College was a baptism by fire. The three years I was at Brooklyn College, 1972–1975, remain a blur: on-the-job political education, rallies on the quad, take-overs, and an arrest. We knew, of course, that the field of ethnic studies was a direct challenge to the conventional academic canon. By suggesting that there might be other sources of knowledge and ways of thinking, we posed an existential threat to higher education's Eurocentric curriculum and traditional ways of doing things. Bilingual education too was a threat because it challenged the "English-Only" ideology that had a stranglehold on the nation – and still does – suggesting that languages other than English were an impediment to academic and life success. It is no exaggeration to say that our department was in constant danger of being eliminated. As I wrote in my memoir,

> New and critical voices were contesting the previously agreed-upon notion of what it meant to be an educated person. No longer limited to

Shakespeare, Faulkner, and Hemingway, the new curricula included Morrison, Neruda, and de Burgos. History was no longer simply about the conquests and achievements of Europeans and Americans; it now included the study of imperialism, colonialism, and exploitation as well.

(Nieto, 2015, p. 176)

The three years I was at Brooklyn College were exhilarating and terrifying at the same time. Participating in rallies, signing petitions, speaking at demonstrations (which is where I honed my speaking skills, not at conferences as is usually the case), and serving as a member of various negotiating committees with the administration; these were all part of the job. Those years also taught me a great deal about the theory and practice of bilingual education and the history of the Puerto Rican community in the United States. In addition, I learned how to prepare course syllabi, teach college courses, and advise students. But what I did not learn in my time at Brooklyn College were the other typical expectations of academic life: I never wrote a journal article or grant, and I presented at only one academic conference in the three years I was there. Those skills had to wait until I began my doctoral studies at UMass and, later, when I became a faculty member there.

Doctoral Studies and a New Awakening

Moving to Massachusetts to begin my doctoral studies in 1975, I faced a different world from my years at Brooklyn College. The Civil Rights Movement was waning and activism was dying down, but remnants of the demands for social justice were still evident, especially in the academic and intellectual realms in which I now found myself. As a doctoral student, the very first course I took, Foundations of Multicultural Education, taught by Professor Bob Suzuki, would define my life's work. In Bob's class and others, I read the early work of James Banks and Geneva Gay, the first books of Jonathan Kozol, and the even earlier work of Horace Mann, W. E. B. DuBois, Horace Kallen, and Carter G. Woodson, among others. Other courses introduced me to Sylvia Ashton-Warner, Howard Zinn, Michael Apple, Joel Spring, Maxine Greene, and others. I was also fortunate to take a course with Sam Bowles and Herb Gintis, faculty members in the Economics Department at the University of Massachusetts (UMass), just before their groundbreaking study *Schooling in Capitalist America* (1976) was published. It was also at UMass that I was introduced to Paulo Freire, both in his writings (1970), and later, in person when he was a visiting scholar on several occasions. I was fortunate to help organize his visits and accompany him to various venues.

Through the work of these and other scholars, I began to understand more deeply than ever that public education, though a noble ideal, rather than "level the playing field," often served instead to exacerbate inequalities, particularly around race, ethnicity, social class, language, and other differences. The work of these theorists, and others, influenced my work as a teacher educator. Reading Antonio Gramsci's work also had a powerful impact on me. His theory of hegemony, the process by which dominant groups create and maintain social control over others, made me question meritocracy, the presence of a "colorblind society," and other such myths. Before beginning my stint at Brooklyn College, I had also fallen victim to the beliefs that we Puerto Ricans spoke an inferior Spanish, that our culture and history had little of value, and that we, in fact, had no history. The Puerto Rican Studies Department at Brooklyn College had disabused me of such ideas. My time as a UMass doctoral student reinforced my growing awareness that these ideas had no merit, while also giving me fresh hope in the power of education as a liberating project.

In 1980, with a freshly minted doctorate and a bunch of ideas on how to make a difference in the lives of marginalized youths and in public education in general, I began my job as an assistant professor at UMass. Teaching preservice and practicing teachers to challenge conventional wisdom and be critical educators, and also introducing them to the benefits of bilingual education, antiracist multicultural education, and later, culturally responsive pedagogy, became instrumental in my work as a teacher educator throughout my time at UMass.

Teacher Education and Academic Life

Despite the fact that I had been a faculty member in Brooklyn College for three years before beginning my doctoral studies, I still felt like an apprentice in my new academic position. My work in the Puerto Rican Studies Department had been more about political struggle, not the typical trajectory of a new scholar. I was designing and teaching courses, mentoring students, presenting at conferences and beginning – finally! – my research agenda. But I was still feeling I had to prove myself as a Puerto Rican scholar and defend multicultural education as a legitimate field of study and research. All of these activities and the constant conflicting emotions about my new role made my first years as an assistant professor challenging on many levels.

Even though my light skin privilege opened doors for me, my gender and young age did not. I remember my first (and what I thought would be my last) experience at the 1980 conference of the American Educational Research Association (AERA). At the time, AERA was an overwhelmingly White and male organization. I went with my mentor, Bob Sinclair, to present my dissertation research, which had focused on the involvement of Puerto Rican families in curriculum development for bilingual programs (it was ironic that the idea of parent involvement I had questioned years earlier had become the major focus of my dissertation research). I still remember the color rising to my face in anger as the discussant on the panel dismissed as foolish the idea of Puerto Rican parents contributing to curricula, saying that such parents – by which I understood he meant immigrants, poorly educated, living in poverty, and non-English speaking – could not possibly know anything about curricula. I swore never to return to AERA.

In spite of this experience, I became an active member of my academic program and department, as well as of the university community. In the early 1980s, when I was a fairly new assistant professor, I was named to the university's Curriculum Committee. It was there that we developed the first diversity requirement at UMass, one of the first in the nation. The policy required all undergraduate students to take at least two courses designated as having "diversity" content. Thinking back on it now, it does not sound like much, but at the time, it was. Even some of the more liberal members of the Curriculum Committee were not convinced of the wisdom of this policy. I recall one of them suggesting that the policy should stipulate that African American students could not use courses in the Afro-American Studies Department as part of their diversity requirement, and that women also would not be able to count courses in Women's Studies as part of the diversity requirement. I made the case, convincingly I think, that *all* students should get credit for taking such courses. Given the monocultural curriculum of K-12 education, I argued that being African American did not necessarily mean one knew anything about African American history, and being a woman did not mean one knew much about patriarchy, except of course, on a lived, practical level. I knew this from my own experience as a Puerto Rican. I believe it was because of my arguments and, indeed, my very presence on that committee that the suggested stipulation was rejected. This is why people of Color make a difference in academia: not because we are necessarily smarter or more knowledgeable than others (although that may be true as well), but rather because our positionalities, our very marginalization and lived experiences give us different lenses with which to view the world.

I should also mention that I did in fact return to AERA, though it took me nine years to do so. It was only when my friend Professor María Torres-Guzmán, then an assistant professor beginning her long tenure at Teachers College, was to be honored as a Distinguished Young Scholar by the committee then called the AERA Committee on the Role and Status of Minorities in Educational Research (since renamed the Committee on Scholars of Color). How could I not attend? When I went to the activity, I was stunned to look around and see the number of people of Color in attendance, a huge change from my first AERA experience. It was an inspiring moment, especially as the awardees were announced. The senior scholar honored that day was the distinguished educator Doxey Wilkerson, a pioneer in civil rights and early childhood education. The look of pride on his face as he received the award was touching. At the time, he was already 84 years old, having waited a lifetime to be so acknowledged. He died in 1993. After that experience, I began to think that perhaps there *was* a place for people like me in AERA. It was that experience that brought me back, and has kept me returning for almost 30 years.

We Matter in Academia and in Teacher Education

The experience of serving on the Curriculum Committee reaffirmed for me how important it is to have people of diverse backgrounds in an academic setting. And my return to AERA taught me that we do indeed make a difference. When I compare what AERA is now to what it was 30-odd years ago, I am amazed. The same can be said about other education organizations. This is not to say that people of Color are always embraced or acknowledged in these organizations; far from it. But our work has made an enormous difference in research as well as in how university students are prepared to become teachers. It is rare nowadays to find a college of education that does not claim social justice as part of its mission. Talking the talk, of course, is quite different from walking the walk, but there is at least a tacit recognition now of the significance of identity and diversity in teaching and learning. There is even a growing (though often grudging) acknowledgment of how racism and inequality have defined education for generations of students of Color and those living in poverty.

As I was to find out through my teaching, not only are we important in university committees where policy is set, but also in other areas of higher education. For example, when a group of students commandeered the Chancellor's Office at UMass in 1985 demanding that the university live up to its commitment of almost a decade earlier to divest from all companies doing business in South Africa, the students asked that a group of five faculty members work with them to negotiate with the administration. I was honored to be one of the faculty members asked. (In 1996, President Nelson Mandela, by then a universally accepted and inspirational international leader, received an honorary doctorate from UMass.) I was also heartened when a number of years later, an activist student referred to me in a newspaper article as "a magnet for students of Color" on our campus.

Besides our research and publishing, it is especially in our courses that teacher educators of Color make a difference. I taught at UMass for 26 years, mostly loving my classes and my students, although occasionally having frustrating and challenging experiences. Over the years, I grew right along with my students, becoming more critical, more knowledgeable, and I hope, wiser and more compassionate as well. Teaching about race and racism, privilege and power, difference and inequality; these are not easy topics. I was lucky that I did not often face hostile students; Massachusetts is, in general, a liberal state where ideas that challenge bias, racism, and privilege are not as shocking or difficult to handle as in other parts of the country. Nonetheless, I found myself more than once facing teary White students feeling guilty and having a hard time accepting that racism still exists, that they have unearned privilege, that not everyone has had the same opportunity as they have, and so on. Students of Color, on the other hand, were often bewildered and angry at what they perceived as the insincere innocence and ignorance of their White peers.

Still happening today 2022

A crucial lesson I learned in my many years in academia is that the demands on us – people of Color, women, GLBTQ faculty, and others marginalized in society – are far greater than those faced by others in academia. We are expected to represent all those who are like us, to be on all committees concerning diversity, to teach everything having to do with race and difference, to mentor all the students of our own backgrounds – while also doing all the work required of every other academic. Consequently, I served as an external reviewer for more than my fair share of tenure and promotion cases because I felt it was my responsibility to support young scholars of Color and defend my academic field. And I do not know how many times I agreed to accept one more – *just one more, please!* – student in my overenrolled courses because they were desperate to take a course that would be meaningful to them. It was a lot to expect and, most of the time, I did it willingly and with enthusiasm. I Thank you You are Brave.

Identity matters, yes, but it should not be the sole responsibility of those of us with the least power and representation in academia to take on these tasks. Given our nation's growing diversity and the fact that children of Color now make up the majority of students in our public schools, more White faculty and faculty of other diverse identities also have to step up to the plate. Creating welcoming and diverse colleges of education and preparing all teachers to be supportive, creative, and critical educators should be everyone's business. When we reach the point where all faculty members in education, and indeed in all departments across universities, acknowledge and act on this responsibility as part of their job, we will have made a visible commitment to the growing calls for social justice in our schools, communities, and nation.

A Belated "Thank You"

No one forges the road by herself. I was fortunate to have several noteworthy role models along the way without whose help and model of perseverance I would not be here today. One was María Engracia Sánchez, one of my colleagues in the Puerto Rican Studies Department and a pioneer in bilingual education in New York City. She was, before Sonia Sotomayor popularized the phrase many years later, a "wise Latina." Another was Antonia Pantoja, a hero to many in the Puerto Rican community because of her fierce advocacy for education and self-determination for our people. Not only was Pantoja a founding member of several organizations aimed at improving the life chances of Puerto Ricans and other Latin@s in the United States, but she also made an indelible contribution to the field of education. In 1996, she was awarded the Presidential Medal of Freedom by President Bill Clinton, at the time the only Puerto Rican woman to be so honored.

And now, as a senior scholar, my new role models are the growing numbers of young Latin@ and other scholars who have taken up the mantle of social justice through their research, teaching, and advocacy. Addressing race and diversity of all kinds, as well as privilege and power, they will continue to make a difference in our communities and for our children.

References

Bowles, S., & Gintis, H. (1976). *Schooling in Capitalist America: Economic reform and the contradictions of economic life*. New York, NY: Basic Books.
Freire, P. (1970). *Pedagogy of the Oppressed*. New York, NY: Seabury Press.
Nieto, S. (2015). *Brooklyn Dreams: My life in public education*. Cambridge, MA: Harvard Education Press.

3 The Transformative Lives We Lead

Making Teacher Education Ours

Patrick Roz Camangian

Many critically conscious teachers and teachers of Color leave the K-12 classroom to pursue careers as teacher educators. Too often, however, they find themselves disappointed with the racial hostility they are faced with when they eventually take on positions at their respective institutions. This disappointment seems daunting and many of these teacher educators remain passive as they wait to presumably transform these spaces when they secure tenure, or a critical mass of like-minded, anti-oppressive colleagues somehow increases. These are some of the recurring messages teacher educators raise to me when seeking advice about confronting White supremacy at their universities. Listening to their dilemmas, and reflecting on my own experiences as a teacher educator, always raises some interesting questions for me. What does it mean to navigate our realities as racially humanizing teacher educators? Does antiracist teacher education only happen when our colleagues support our efforts in ways that we think they should? In other words, does socially transformative teacher education only happen after the conditions that trouble us are resolved? Or, does how we respond to the racial contradictions facing us help shape the experiences we have? When I started my career, the University of San Francisco (USF) felt very much like a traditional, private, Catholic, Jesuit, and predominantly White, institution. Like many teacher educators, I experienced the job as socially toxic. In this chapter, though, I share my experiences in hopes that I can address some of the concerns raised above.

I identify as a working class and anti-imperial Filipino male in the North American, West Coast diaspora. Prior to my career as a teacher educator, I was not always committed to education or critically conscious of this identity. Back in 1989 – when I was 15 years old – I was pushed out of high school early during my tenth grade year for cutting weeks of classes, failing every course, and starting a gang-related rumble in the middle of the quad during lunch. I tried my hand at continuation school, but after that very short stint, I found myself drifting the streets for the next seven years of my life. I passed my proficiency exam when I was eighteen and I began trudging through community college. In summer 1996, my most profound education began as an OG – original gangster: a term respectfully ascribed to elder gang members – educated me to the fact that the high proportion of people of Color in prisons, especially Raza and Africans, or Black and Brown folks, was because "we" were doing exactly what this system wanted us to do. This conversation helped me make critical sense of how joining my "homeboys" in the "street life" made us complicit in our own oppression.

After reflecting on the reality of what the above experience meant, I realized that for a large part of my life I had no purpose – I was chillin' on the block, drinking and smoking daily, looking for fights and disrespecting women for sport, and hating people who looked phenotypically just like me. For a time, I deemed my history of alienation from school as a deficiency. I was caught up in the hegemony. This epiphany later helped me more effectively problematize this in my teaching of high school students and has since helped me understand more intimately what is required when preparing teachers to support young people in navigating the material conditions of their everyday lives. Young people in historically oppressed communities are disproportionately exposed to inequitable social conditions, and interrelated racial hatred, that often lead to uninformed decisions and displaced anger (Fanon, 1963). I draw on these experiences to teach preservice teachers the motivating power of counter-hegemonic discursive spaces for youth of Color. If we as teacher educators truly want to be more effective with teaching teachers of urban youth, then we have to prepare our preservice candidates to channel their students' energy against the very social conditions that undermine their existence. In this way, I try to teach teachers how to scaffold critical deconstructions of Western imperialism with urban youth's often scathing critique of society in academically empowering ways (see Camangian, 2015).

I further developed the anti-imperialist framework introduced to me by the OG by studying, organically, how the Filipina/o diaspora had great relevance to all people struggling for self-determination. Grounded in poor and working class perspectives, I found lessons in the legacy of resistance in the Philippines from, and for, our people that I continue to draw inspiration, strength, and root my practice in to this day. As an early career assistant professor, I maintained my connections with different pro-people, anti-imperial organizing spaces as well as other teacher organizations outside of the university. Broadly speaking, pro-people politics are grounded in the idea that social transformation should be led by oppressed people, for oppressed people, and accountable to oppressed people (Rosca & Sison, 2004). Organizing in Los Angeles' Filipino community, then in various teacher-organizing spaces served as the foundation upon which I would build my pedagogical practice on all levels moving forward. Not only did I learn about revolutionary concepts through study, I was able to apply my learning through actual community practice. Applying what we learn from critical social theory to how we engage students, communities, and schools is fundamental to developing a critical race and class analysis that resonates with the very people we seek to serve as educators. Not applying theory to practice, critically conscious educators and teacher educators – even if from racially subjugated or working class backgrounds – too often anchor their worldview on the theory. Thus, their sense of social transformation is very abstract and often misses its connection with the practice and the people needed to actually transform oppressive conditions.

During my first year as a faculty member at USF, I was faced with a White elitist context that made me call into question my purpose as an academic, scholar, and activist. The student demographic in the Teacher Education Department (TED) in which I worked was roughly 70% White, 15% Latina/o, and 13% Asian. The cultural and ideological climate in our program was incongruent with the material needs of the communities that the university was purportedly honoring in its rhetoric. The mere presence of 30% non-White students did not make USF's TED feel more humanizing. I felt out of place, and despite some students phenotypically looking familiar to the people in the communities I was coming from, it was clear that they had a different class identity.

Midway through my first year at USF during the 2008–2009 academic year, I began to plot the transformation of my experience at USF by connecting with others. Unlike the community work I have been involved with, the critical mass of like-minded people in my department was small. Connecting with Professor Noah Borrero seemed like a natural collaboration. Together, we re-established a program similar to the one built by Herb Kohl at USF in the late 1990s called the Center for Teaching Excellence and Social Justice. This program had been discontinued as the department, overall, had felt that this center's predominantly critical educator of Color cohort model was exclusive. Building on Borrero's expertise in bilingualism and my background in critical pedagogy, we combined our experiences to develop the Masters in Urban Education and Social Justice (UESJ) program for TED. Along the way, we recruited radical-left activist Rick Ayers and Deep East Oakland English and Raza Studies teacher Sharim Hannegan-Martinez to teach in our program and to build critical mass in the very limited space available for us to create this change.

To establish a base of racially, culturally, and politically diverse students at USF, through UESJ, we actively tried to identify, recruit, and train more teacher candidates who came from the communities UESJ aims to serve and who genuinely respected and honored the lives of urban youth. One of the first things I did when co-coordinating UESJ was to spread the word about the program, visiting different local community centers and schools, speaking at California universities, and being proactive with our recruitment. I was pounding the pavement. Rather than silence my identity and mute my urban sensibilities, I leveraged my unique background and critical pedagogical perspective to recruit other much-needed educator of Color voices to our program. As a historically working class Filipino and former gang member who did not take the traditional path to higher education, how I express and embody my identity makes a lot of difference to the teacher candidates and aspiring educators who I recruit, teach, and mentor. My frank, scathing critique of dominant society resonated with the recruits of Color I was connecting with at deep, cultural, and community levels. Rather than temper my tongue, the passion I embodied, profanity I indicted with, and stories I evoked piqued a lot of interest in the type of candidates I tried to recruit.

My volunteering as a classroom teacher in Oakland also drew attention to UESJ as we became one of the only urban education credential and masters programs with a laboratory classroom, run by a professor, on the West Coast, if not the country. Through this laboratory classroom, I was able to apply the pedagogical theories we were developing to classroom practice while also providing an apprenticeship model for recruits interested in learning to teach under my tutelage. To date, 18 UESJ students have apprenticed as teachers in training. This has also helped in recruiting for the UESJ program, as visitors have come to observe me teach and inquire about the possibilities of studying at USF. This presence in East Oakland schools is often respected for building a pipeline for conscious folks of Color who want to be teachers. Other critically conscious non-Whites, White allies, and activist applicants are drawn to USF's UESJ because they are familiar with our commitment and purpose. Since my participation eight years ago, of the 140 students we have admitted, 70% have been students of Color.

Recruiting candidates from similar material conditions of urban youth radically shifts the way our candidates think about serving students of Color. We also require that White admits have experience doing some level of critically conscious work. Drawing politically conscious students from the abovementioned spaces is critical in shifting the paradigm that students in UESJ must grapple with. Further, this type of diversity – beyond cultural and phenotypical traits – also disrupts the discourse in the larger teacher educational spaces that normalize whiteness, White supremacy, and class hostility toward urban youth and youth of Color. UESJ students with higher levels of critical consciousness are able to, then, draw on their experiences in urban communities to add insights into classroom conversations that a large majority of teacher credential students cannot. In other words, they add so much value to USF classes that typically lack insights into the urban classrooms that we are preparing them for.

The presence of critically conscious candidates of Color and White allies emboldened to defend themselves and their perspectives against the dominant, deficit perspectives of White candidates both inside of UESJ and TED raised the ire of my TED colleagues. So much of these colleagues' frustration was based on feelings that general TED students were being verbally attacked by UESJ students whenever the former's problematic, however innocent, statements were being made. The majority of faculty in TED named the supposed lack of collegiality practiced by UESJ students as hostile, harmful, and unwarranted. This tension was projected onto our stability as TED faculty. As a result, Noah and I began to feel like the continuation of UESJ as a TED program was vulnerable to the sentiments felt by our colleagues. The conservative, bourgeois, and White-male-dominated culture of the larger School of Education (SOE) intensified our trepidation even further. We did not feel in control of our future, or the future of our program, as early career professors.

Rather than exist at the behest of the existing racial, cultural, and ideological climate of the SOE, we believed that we had a responsibility to operationalize a paradigm shift. The institutional space was oppositional to discussions about social transformation, and progressive educational policy and practice. We drew on our research, and expertise in race, class, and gender equity, and my background in pro-people, anti-imperial organizing described above to inform my work as a teacher educator in this space.

Drawing on both my research and organizing practice informed my work with others outside of the TED to collectively create the conditions necessary to increase our sphere of influence inside my department, and throughout the SOE. Increasing my sphere of influence in this way helped protect the work we were doing inside of TED, and reframe UESJ as the type of work that was honoring the mission and vision of the university. During my third year, I began to connect with the very few other like-minded faculty members in other departments to build a more politically informed movement in SOE. We convened a series of small, informal meetings where we each talked about our struggles and what we were doing about it as critically conscious faculty members. Most of our interventions, we found, were at the curricular level in our courses. Our conversations grew more meaningful, and started to be grounded in actual strategies to transform the existing SOE space altogether. The plan for the progression of our conversations was to bring additional allies in the fold.

Our dialogue led us to strategizing ways in which each of us were going to assume leadership positions across our different departments, in SOE faculty leadership, and on committees that served our interests to advance the ways in which we were interpreting the university's social justice values. I assumed the role of co-chairing the professional development committee. This small group of critically conscious professors assumed positions of leadership and used these to leverage the mission and vision of the university to shift the conservative discourse that had prevailed for decades.

We anticipated colleagues with reactionary politics who were accustomed to dominating discussions with deficit perspectives to push back on our progressive leanings. To offset this, a tactic we used was for one of us to assume the responsibility to resist them openly, and unapologetically, challenging anything we believed to be problematic. We knew we needed to be organized. If we anticipated 10 problematic voices, we identified 10 voices of resistance to push back, with more waiting in the wings in case we needed it. We also needed different voices addressing the various issues we were looking to advance across all the spaces we were participating in. These drawn-out efforts led to hiring faculty, and even high-ranking SOE leadership, whose research and practice we believed to be in-line with the ways in which we interpreted the mission and vision of the university and whose body of work was more aligned with the needs of the local poor and working class communities the SOE had long ignored.

Transforming our conditions in this way helped make our institution more open to progressive interpretations of socially just work. This paradigm shift in the school helped positively recognize UESJ as a go-to program for preparing teachers committed to urban education. Instead of being a lone voice of resistance in TED, I became a central voice among other organized faculty who were now being seen and treated as leaders in the larger SOE. What was once being treated as a marginal, even disposable, program is now being embraced by colleagues across all departments and being held up by SOE leadership as the model for other programs in the school to aspire toward.

My point, essentially, is that socially transformative teacher education does not come *after* the contradictions have been confronted – it comes hand and hand with it. Implied in so many questions asked about how we can do radical work in reactionary spaces are defeatist perspectives. It is grounded in thoughts like, "If I did not have to deal with conservative students then I could really do socially transformative teacher education." Or, "If I had a department or Dean that was concerned with issues of justice then I could really thrive as a teacher educator." I know that I have the privilege of making this critique from a more liberal regional context, but I do not think these are very inspiring perspectives to assume. As socially transformative educators and teacher educators, we will always be faced with inequities and resistances.

It makes sense in our alienation to critique the ways in which the professional conditions constrain our teacher educator lives. I understand why we decide to disengage from our departments, and our students, and our institutions because they are not what we idealized them to be prior to finding ourselves there. The truth is, our contexts will long be imperfect. When we find ourselves in circumstances and conditions that are unfavorable to our struggle, our job is not to find ways to be maladjusted to the social suffering inside our profession. Contradictions, and challenges, in our profession will forever come our way. I think it is often the case that we think we are being anti-oppressive by identifying and analyzing the inequitable aspects of our jobs, but when we do not commit to applying this analysis to actual transformation then we are simply contributing to the existing inequities. Our responsibility, instead, is to work collectively to transform our institutions so that they are less hostile to our humanity, our practice, and our purpose. This must be the transformative teacher education life we lead.

References

Camangian, P. (2015). Teaching like lives depend on it: Agitate, arouse, inspire. *Urban Education, 50*(4), 424–453.

Fanon, F. (1963). *The Wretched of the Earth*. New York, NY: Grove.

Rosca, N., & Sison, J. M. (2004). *Jose Maria Sison: At home in the world – Portrait of a revolutionary*. Greensborough, NC: Open Hand Publishing.

4 Tales From the Dark Side

Reflections of Blackness and Maleness in Teacher Education

Tyrone C. Howard

I was enlightened to the realities of my work as a Black male teacher educator (BMTE) at the end of my first quarter of teaching a teacher education course at a large university in the Midwest. A White woman who was a student in the class completed her course survey, and waited a few minutes after the class to speak with me. After everyone left she took the time to share with me how much she enjoyed the class, how much she learned and how challenging the content was on a weekly basis. The conversation took a strange twist when the student also commented, "I'm glad that it all worked out, because in the beginning, we didn't know what to make of you." Much to my curiosity I probed what she meant by the statement. She clumsily explained that many of the students in the class were a bit surprised "to see a man" teaching their first course in a teacher education program. She commented that they wondered if I had ever taught before. If so, was I a good teacher? Could I teach women how to teach?

As my curiosity in the conversation grew I asked the student whether, along with questions and uncertainties about my gender being an issue in preparing teachers, my being Black was a topic of discussion as well. The student paused, began to turn a beet-red as she contemplated how to respond to what I presumed was a very straightforward question and replied "well um, ah yes that came up too." As I asked the student to explain further, she stated, "Most of us have never had a Black professor." As the student stammered to talk about the firsts of having a Black male professor, in teacher education no less, it became apparent that there was an undercurrent dialogue about my positionality as a BMTE. I asked the student whether or not students had similar conversations about their White female professors to which she replied, "no, not really. It's just assumed that they get it." That exchange has remained with me as I continue to work in teacher education as a Black man. There is an underlying assumption for many of my students that as they prepare to teach in increasingly diverse classrooms, their White women professors "get it," and individuals like myself do not, until proven otherwise and hopefully it all "works out."

This book is a perfectly timed contribution to a silenced dialogue that is long overdue where issues of teacher education, race, identity and positionality are concerned. Perhaps more than ever, the manner in which we think about, and do the work of preparing the next generation of teachers is critical to recognizing that who we are as teacher educators matters. Parker Palmer (2007) in his insightful work, *The Courage to Teach* says, "We teach who we are" (p. 22). Thus, the question for each and every teacher educator is "*Who am I?*" And how does who I am influence the manner in which I do work in preparing teachers? What unique set of skills, knowledge, experiences and dispositions do I possess that can adequately prepare teachers to work in increasingly diverse schools? And perhaps, most importantly, how does my identity shape, or even minimize, hurt, or hinder how teacher candidates receive that information? What cannot be lost in the process of who we are as teacher educators is that, as our students are trying to make sense of us, our multiple social identities (race, class, gender, sexual orientation, political disposition) influence the manner in which we do this work.

BMTE Positionality

I learned early on, that as a BMTE, these identities pose some very unique challenges in doing the work of preparing teachers, especially in an environment where a majority of the individuals who are pursuing teaching nationally are White women, most of whom are monolingual and from middle class backgrounds (Landsman & Lewis, 2011). I have typically been the only Black male in teacher education programs where I have taught. To that end, when I walk into a class on the first day I am mindful of my maleness, my blackness, and even my body composition (6'4" close to 200 lbs) and what that represents in a classroom where most of the students are women, and while working in the Midwest they were mostly White women. I have personally had to experience White female students inquiring about my physical presence (how tall are you?), compliments about my physical appearance and dress that I have to downplay. And at all costs, I am mindful to avoid any physical contact with students; whereas I see my White female colleagues often embrace students or playfully touch them, those are a no-no for me.

Any suggestions of Black male–White female interactions are situated in a troublesome history about power, gender, allegations of rape, and perceived sexual prowess and promiscuity. While teaching at a university in the Midwest I had to be ever aware of the long, sordid, and complicated history of Black men and White women. The objectification of Black males' bodies through a White prism was prevalent during slavery, wherein Black men who were lynched often had their genitals mutilated. I have to constantly be aware of how notions of implicit bias influence the way that many Whites see people of Color (Blanton & Jaccard, 2008). Moreover, I have to be conscious of how these notions of bias have a more deleterious effect on Black people and Black men in particular (Howard, 2013).

I have also had White women students ask me "what should we call you?" To which I have replied "what do you call your White professors?" I have had teacher candidates question whether or not I have ever taught (which I have), where I taught, where I went to school, and in some cases, experienced sheer looks of curiosity and confusion when seeing me enter the class on the first day. In short, there is often an ongoing assessment of whether or not I am qualified to do this work that my White colleagues are not subjected to. The irony in this sizing up of me and other people of Color is that it occurs as many preservice teachers are preparing to work in urban communities where a growing number of the students that they will teach look like me, or come from communities where I grew up and teach; while many of their White professors are much less likely to be equipped to help them to understand the realities of the communities, schools, and students that they will teach.

There are many ways in which the unique and oftentimes untold perspectives of BMTEs can help move the field forward, particularly in the understanding of ideology, pedagogy, and practices that could support Black male students, and other males of Color who are increasingly one of the most disenfranchised affinity groups in public schools (Conchas, 2006; Howard, 2014). According to Lewis and Toldson (2013), Black men make up only 1.8% of all teachers in the U.S., and the percentage of Black men in teacher education is considered to be even smaller. Since BMTEs have successfully navigated the academic path from kindergarten to college and beyond, many of us are better able to identify and disseminate the academic and social strategies used by many Black male students and other males of Color to effectively plot a course through schools. My experience in this work has been both challenging and rewarding; it has been frustrating and fulfilling. Frustrating because there has been in the past a need to consistently prove myself worthy to teach certain teacher education students; fulfilling when they recognize that there are contributions that I can add that they may not gain anywhere else. What is critical to this work is the constant reflection of my own race, gender, experiences, and other identity markers, as well as those of my students. Make no doubt about it; this is a constant and iterative process.

Insights of BMTEs

One of the issues that are queried when examining issues of race and gender in teacher education is whether or not there are certain skills, knowledge, and dispositions that I possess as a BMTE that my colleagues who are not Black male do not possess. The answer is complex and multifaceted, but in my opinion an emphatic YES. There are ways of knowing, doing, and being as a BMTE that I possess that I think are crucial for preparing teachers, especially for those who are getting ready to teach in racially and culturally diverse school settings. These explanations provide validation for why there is a pressing need for more Black men in teaching and more specifically teacher education.

As a Black man I can speak of challenges overcome, obstacles conquered, and educational goals that have been accomplished when I come from a group where school success is not the norm, but the exception. I can speak of how and when race and racism accusations are real when it comes to how many Black males experience schooling. Over the past several years, the inexcusable numbers of unarmed Black men being killed at the hands of police informs my pedagogy.

Many preservice and inservice teachers adopt colorblind approaches to their teaching. A number of scholars have documented the dangers in using such approaches (Bonilla-Silva, 2006). To that end, when I discuss colorblindness with teachers, I remind them that while they may insist they do not see race (which I completely reject), the wider society sees young Black and Brown boys through a racial prism. Moreover, the fact that young men and boys like Michael Brown, Trayvon Martin, and Tamir Rice were all unarmed and killed, shapes the manner in which many young Black boys and boys of Color think about their own survival, their own racial make up, and the manner in which others see them. So, in short, when teachers claim race is not significant, yet for young Black boys it *is* significant, to deny it is quite dismissive of their realities. Discussion of such topics can be further informed from a Black man's perspective, and cannot be overlooked. I am able to help teachers and teaching candidates understand how and why young men of Color disengage from or resist schooling and society writ large.

I cannot profess to be an expert on all things that occur in education for each and every young Black male, but I can offer insight into the minds, behaviors, hearts, and souls of many young Black and Brown men, because they, much like I did, are searching to belong, looking to be valued and affirmed in classrooms, are seeking an identity, and are trying to navigate the complex terrain of schooling while still remaining whole and human in the process. I can relate to the frustration of growing up Black and male in an urban community where issues of violence, death, despair, and hopelessness are permanent residents. I can identify with the pain that comes when teachers assume that they are the culprit of wrong deeds done in the classroom, or how they immediately become the suspect if someone's belongings are suddenly missing, or the deep suspicion that arises when they do well academically. In short, I have walked on a path similar to the paths of many young Black males today, and can begin to articulate what they feel, why they feel it, and offer the best approaches to address it in a compassionate, caring, yet humane manner that can assist young Black males in feeling as if they belong, they are normal, and that school success is within their grasp as much as it is for any other group of students.

While I do believe that White teacher educators can effectively talk about and teach to race (Sleeter, 2015), my experience is that most of my White colleagues are only able to superficially address topics related to race. As a BMTE, I possess an ability to engage preservice teachers with in-depth discussions about how racism manifests itself in a multitude of ways. I often discuss with my students that when, not if, race-related topics arise in their classrooms that they have to be prepared to listen, learn, and to try to empathize with the stories that are told by students of Color. I can speak to them about how the pervasiveness of race and racism can lead to many students thinking that any slight presence of differential treatment could be due to racial discrimination, even when it is not. I am able to help my students hear and know why colorblind approaches can be harmful in their discussions with students, and that their refusal to acknowledge and validate racial realities can be a huge mistake in terms of connecting to their students and affirming their identities and experiences. I am equipped to help preservice teachers understand how even well-intentioned teachers can be persistently complicit in racial microaggressions which can have a profound influence on the way that students of Color experience schools (Kohli & Solórzano, 2012). I must be clear that these are approaches that work for me as a BMTE, but by no means do I want to suggest that all Black men, nor all people of Color, can effectively have these discussions, but I have been able to develop an approach and skill set that fosters these conversations taking place.

Sharing of the Self

The work of teacher education can be deeply personal and reflective, wherein candidates have to build on their experiences as learners, and of teachers who made an impact on their lives. To that end, one of the tasks that I frequently ask my students to engage in is a race/class/gender autobiography. The purpose of the assignment is to think, read, reflect, write, and ultimately speak about multiple identities. I typically start this activity by sharing my own story, and modeling how I experienced race as a child; was profiled repeatedly because of my race in ways that education could not eradicate. I also share with my students how internalized notions of racism can manifest in ways that caused me to question my intellect, doubt my abilities, and wonder about my potential to be successful. These conversations around race are to let my teacher education students know that race can have a profound influence on the students that they teach; that for many students of Color it is their primary sense of self, and the lens through which they see the world and they often believe the world sees them.

I also interrogate my male privilege and how I have operated with blinders for many years, not realizing how patriarchy manifests itself in everyday practices, and how I need to be mindful of that privilege and listen to the experiences, struggles, and encounters that women face. I also address growing up in a working class, urban neighborhood, where people played by the rules of the game yet still made little-to-no progress. I share with them how watching people who live in dire circumstances brought on by poverty did not diminish their spirit to thrive, or their determination to be better, and how education is often viewed as a lifeline for children and families in such situations. I walk my students through this process because I want them to experience the discomfort of talking about race, the awkwardness of discussing their class privilege, or even sharing their comfort in addressing how as women (for most of my students) they encountered far too many instances of sexual harassment, gender bias, or differential treatment based on their sex or gender. Taking on such activities is done in my teacher education courses to help candidates realize how identities are deeply political, as is the nature of teaching. I also want them to learn the value of reflection, and to engage in it on a regular basis, and the benefits that can emerge pedagogically and professionally in the process (Howard, 2003).

Recommendations for Preparing Teachers to Work with Males of Color

To sum up, I end with some strategies or steps that can be used to educate Black males or other males of Color. My first point of insight is to understand that the group is not monolithic. Not all males of Color play or even enjoy sports. Also, be aware that while a hip-hop based pedagogy may work for some, it may be completely foreign or of no interest to others. To this end, avoid the generalizable one-size-fits-all approach. I usually tell my teacher education students that my experiences as a Black male can be completely at odds with another Black male's, and it is their job as educators to get to know each of their students at the most human level that they can to develop and cultivate meaningful relationships with them.

Next, I argue that authenticity matters. This applies for all students, but I would contend that for many males of Color, teacher authenticity is crucial, and any efforts that come across as superficial or patronizing will be quickly criticized and alter teacher–student relationships. I strongly encourage my teacher education students to be prepared to make statements such as "I don't know about that," "Can you teach me more about that…" and "Explain to me how that makes you feel…" Such statements can be quite helpful in helping students understand that learning is a reciprocal process and that you see them as teachers as well as learners. Being aware of your limitations concerning students' background, culture, and interests is vital in developing a level of authenticity that garners students' respect and paves the way for genuine connections.

Last, I leave with the notion that intersectionality matters. In preparing teachers it is vital that boys of Color are framed as having multiple identities. There are young men who are biracial, they may be gay or bisexual, or they may be questioning their sexual orientation. It is crucial to also be mindful of young men who are immigrants, or the sons of immigrants, and that this undoubtedly shapes their identities and behaviors. The way that people's lives unfold is always in a state of flux, and ever evolving.

The work of preparing teachers in today's cultural climate can be frightening, worrisome, scary, and at times full of comments, stares, and interpretations that are often inexplicable yet far too common in teacher education programs. My desire in doing the work of preparing teachers is rooted in a deep, authentic, and unyielding commitment to justice and equity. As a BMTE I enter my work hoping that every child, but particularly those on the margins, is able to use education as a passport to the future.

References

Blanton, H., & Jaccard, J. (2008). Unconscious racism: A concept in pursuit of a measure. *Annual Review of Sociology, 34*, 277–297.

Bonilla-Silva, E. (2006). *Racism without Racists: Colorblind racism and the persistence of racial inequality in the United States* (2nd ed.). Lanham, MD: Rowman & Littlefield.

Conchas, G. (2006). *The Color of Success: Race and high-achieving urban youth.* New York, NY: Teachers College Press.

Howard, T. C. (2003). Culturally relevant pedagogy: Ingredients for critical teacher reflection. *Theory into Practice, 42*(3), 195–202.

Howard, T. C. (2013) How does it feel to be a problem? Black male students, schools, and learning in enhancing the knowledge base to disrupt deficit frameworks. *Review of Research in Education, Volume 37*(1), 66–98.

Howard, T. C. (2014). *Black Male(d): Peril and promise in the education of African American males.* New York, NY: Teachers College Press.

Kohli, R., & Solórzano, D. G. (2012). Teachers, please learn our names!: Racial microaggressions and the K-12 classroom. *Race Ethnicity and Education, 15*(4), 441–462.

Landsman, J., & Lewis, C. (Eds.) (2011). *White Teachers/Diverse Classrooms: Creating inclusive schools, building on students' diversity and providing true educational equity* (2nd ed.). Sterling, VA: Stylus.

Lewis, C. W., & Toldson, I. A. (2013). *Black Male Teachers: Diversifying the workplace.* Bingley, UK: Emerald Group Publishing.

Palmer, P. J. (2007). *The Courage to Teach: Exploring the inner landscape of a teacher's life.* San Francisco, CA: Jossey-Bass.

Sleeter, C. E. (2015). *White Bread: Weaving cultural past into the present.* Rotterdam, Netherlands: Sense Publishers.

5 How Neoliberal Education Reform Injured a StrongBlackprofessor

Mari Ann Banks (Roberts)

> *I love education, knowhatimsayin? But if education ain't elevatin' me… it ain't taking me where I need to go, then fuck education. At least [theirs]. ~ stic.man*
>
> (dead prez, 2000)

I am a teacher educator from a lineage of African American teachers who have felt a responsibility to uplift the Black race. We have each identified with what Joan Morgan (1999) calls the myth of the strongBlackwoman "who does not have the same fears, weaknesses and insecurities as other women… is able to handle any crisis… and will keep on helping, saving, nurturing, protecting, mentoring, loving, encouraging, leading – making sure everyone's back is covered but her own" (pp. 101–103).

Morgan finds the strongBlackwoman identity problematic because it asks from Black women more than it should, and she writes about her conundrum in embodying and rejecting it simultaneously (ibid., p. 104). I share her struggle. Family members consistently remind me of my duty and legacy as an educator – to make things better for the Black race, to improve the perception of the Black race, and to overtly (and covertly) work for systemic change for the Black race. And our modus operandi? Public Education. I have been told to do this no matter the resistance and I have proudly taken on the role. I guess I will label us strongBlackteachers.

I am an Associate Professor of Multicultural Education in Metro Atlanta. My university is primarily attended by African American, non-traditional, female, lower socio-economic status students. I have been here for seven years and I feel I was called to this place. I am cisgender, and my marginalized intersectional identities, among which are being female with a disability, have only solidified my resolve and connection to my students.

Similar to the experiences of other African American professors, Black students on campus seek my counsel and organizational advisement – whether or not they have been in my classes. Like many strongBlackprofessors over the history of our profession, I consider this service part of my calling as an educator; and I give of myself abundantly (Ladson-Billings, 2005). In much of my limited free time I work to eliminate education policy harmful to students of the global majority[1] through community and professional organizations.

Please understand that I am not easily intimidated. The strongBlackprofessor in me has never shied away from educational challenges. Yet, despite all the dedication and calling I describe above, I am presently *living* stic man's words. I am saddened by how U.S. public education, which should be a lynchpin in gaining parity and equity for all, has been perverted by a perfect storm of standardization, corporatization, and privatization. I am tired of the injury inflicted by "their education." So I have responded by becoming a part-time teacher educator and, soon, I may not even be that.

My strongBlackprofessor identity has wandered the university, a violently displaced refugee looking for a new home. As a result, I now only teach one class and have become director of my university's Center for Academic Success (CAS); a lovely place but, to me, only a place where I will not have to participate in the imbroglio that public teacher education has become. I have largely deserted the occupation I love, replacing it with something that looks and feels like it, but just is not the real thing. The reason for my desertion is exhaustingly complicated yet can be described using only three words – neoliberal education reform.

Neoliberal Education Reform

Neoliberal education reforms have been most evident since the advent of NCLB (the No Child Left Behind Act) in 2001. Many of these reforms (e.g. high-stakes testing, increased standardization, and value-added methods of measuring teacher performance) take precedence in public education, their usual guise involving claims of improving outcomes for marginalized students. Yet, the reforms have actually carpet bombed public education with the most damage being sustained by students of the global majority, the very students reformers claim to assist (Ahlquist, Gorski, & Montaño, 2011; National Center for Fair and Open Testing, 2010; Madeloni & Gorlewski, 2013; Roberts, 2015).

These policy changes are spurred by a group of foundations, corporations, and non-governmental organizations. These entities are led by a culturally homogeneous, interconnected network of wealthy corporate leaders and philanthropists and the politicians and school officials who smooth their path. Diane Ravitch (2010) has labeled many of them the *Billionaire Boys Club* and, identical to stic man's "they," they have joined forces to promote market-driven changes which undermine the fundamental nature of public education. These individuals, or entities to which they are connected, purposely spur neoliberal education reform to derive significant financial benefit and their methodology is closely related to profiteering derived from the Prison Industrial Complex (e.g. Croft, Roberts, & Stenhouse, 2016; Hursh, 2016; Roberts, 2015).

Neoliberal reforms have also oozed into the university, masquerading under names like, "consumer-driven," "move-on-when-ready," and "STEM education for the global economy." Arguably, university neoliberal reform seems most invasive in teacher education. For example, like many teacher educator-scholars, when co-constructing my department's student–teacher evaluation instruments, we put deep, hard work into identifying qualities that make an excellent teacher. Yet, reforms now require us to replace our carefully crafted evaluation instruments with unvalidated, high-stakes, standardized tests (viz., edTPA, Intern Keys) mandated by the state of Georgia (GA). The state has further declared that passing these tests, specifically edTPA, is required for teacher licensure.

Among many objections to the top-down imposition of such an instrument, one primary concern is that mandates to use standardized assessments marginalize teacher educators' knowledge, experience, and scholarship. Our already peripheral status within the academy is challenged as our research and opinions are shunted aside. Worse, teacher educators *allow* this to happen, openly submitting to the destruction of our field; and in some cases, even embracing such. I have always believed that, if challenged, teacher educator-scholars would fight for our profession. Then arose this submissive *nothing* many of us are doing to resist neoliberal education reform… It is incomprehensible, frustrating, and has broken my heart.

Until recently, I have fought back against "their" education in multiple ways. My refusal to implement the edTPA has been adamant, thus subverting my department's mandates and angering some of my colleagues. I have supported my students by helping them write articles about their experiences (Brown, 2015) and involving them in a teach-in regarding push-back against neoliberal education reform. I have written articles, op-eds, poems, chapters, demonstrated at the state house – all to no avail. EdTPA still exists, the neoliberals are still destroying public education and I have no idea how to ethically teach my preservice teachers.

Black Lives Matter When Black Men Teach

As a strongBlackprofessor, I have always felt a particular joy when a dynamic, African American male student says, "I want to be a teacher." Hearing this, I typically begin to rhapsodize about the joys inherent in teaching and the need for young African American children to see positive, familiar, male role models in the classroom. I promise the student, "you may never know how or when – but you *will* make a needed difference for our community." Thus, my strongBlackprofessor identity initially rejoiced when I heard Louis, one of my favorite African American male students, say "I want to be a teacher."

For young Black males, life in the U.S. often consists of traumatizing events that hinder the achievement of positive cultural identity and self-respect, and public education all too frequently results in failure (Noguera, 2009). For example, there are numerous unprovoked deaths of Black youth by law enforcement officers/would-be officiates, many marginalized young men are taking the pain in their lives out on one another in a classic example of Post Traumatic Slave Syndrome (DeGruy, 2005), and the need for people to come together and proclaim, "Black Lives Matter," clearly indicates that for many they do not (Grant, Brown, & Brown, 2016; Yancy & hooks, 2015).

Metro Atlanta contains one of the largest African American populations in the country. Here, I see Black males habitually faced with systemic and institutional oppression. Here, there are overwhelming numbers of female parent-led households and here, while parental absence is only part of the reason, I see young men, without sufficient male role models, making terrible choices ranging from poor grades to murder and drugs (ARC, 2013; Holzman, 2010; Moguldom Media Group, 2014; USDOE Office for Civil Rights, 2014). Yet, more importantly, here I also see African American male role models demonstrating that Black lives do matter as they work to make a positive difference in the lives of Black youth – particularly young men (e.g. 100 Black Men of Atlanta, n.d.).

Latino, Black, Asian, and Native American teachers account for 17% of U.S. public school teachers but Black men make up just 2% of the teaching workforce (Bristol, 2015). Conversely, slightly more than half of all public school students are children of Color, and at least 16% are African American (NCES, 2016). U.S. school districts, acknowledging the importance of cultural congruence in the success of students of Color, have instituted programs to address this disparity (e.g. Layton, 2015). Simply, the U.S. needs Black male teachers.

But, that day, I told Louis *not* to teach.

I did not give this advice because Louis is a weak student; in fact, he is a dynamic, energetic, diligent, intelligent, caring African American male student teacher – the holy grail of my constant teacher recruitment efforts!

What just happened?

I have been struggling with my feelings about public education for some time but, as Louis left my office after our talk, I just sat there – aghast at my advice. While gazing at my office door a pain I had been avoiding took root in my soul. I was forced to acknowledge that I had drifted far from my belief in public education and my strongBlackprofessor had been crippled in the process. Through my experience with neoliberal reform, I had been *morally injured*. And the strongBlackteacher committed to public education who I always *thought* I would be? She had just limped away – dragging my moral compass through the dust.

Moral Injury

Psychologist Brett Litz and his colleagues (2009) have defined moral injury as an outcome of "perpetrating, failing to prevent, bearing witness to, or learning about acts that transgress deeply held moral beliefs and expectations"

(p. 700). The authors discuss moral injury as an integral part/outcome of the post-traumatic stress disorder (PTSD) experienced by military service members who have seen, and may have participated in, activities that violated who they believed themselves to be at their moral core. It is created by an act of transgression that creates dissonance and conflict because it violates assumptions and beliefs about right, wrong, and personal goodness. The authors further argue, if individuals are unable to assimilate or accommodate (integrate) the act of transgression within existing self- and relational schemas, they will experience guilt, shame, anxiety, lingering psychological distress, and engage in avoidance behaviors.

I am not comparing my job as a teacher educator to a soldier's. Thankfully, I have never seen someone violently lose their life. What has given *me* PTSD, however, is the assault, disguised as public education, upon students of the global majority who are losing their lives and futures to a broken and corrupt system.

My moral injury is generated when I see students encounter neoliberal education and I do not, or cannot, stop the insanity. Schools in New York, Chicago, and Atlanta have been closed. Students in GA schools have had recess replaced with test prep and have been told that they are unable to have textbooks and must function from worksheets alone. Student teachers are being forced into a standardized mold that is being called "good teaching." And, most unforgivable, is that these outcomes primarily take place in schools populated by students of the global majority.

As Litz et al.'s (2009) framework requires, I once believed deeply in the potential of public education and understood my place as a moral arbitrator of its process. Now, that belief has been violently dispelled and my disability, clinical depression, has reacted in kind by deepening my despair and making me even more susceptible to this special kind of PTSD. For others, the moral injury "their" education produces, has manifested in suicides, rampant cheating, resigning, and student–teacher protests across the U.S. (Baker, 2012; Edelman, Jamieson, & Schram, 2015; Gonzalez, 2016; Rivera, 2013). Teacher Lauren Porosoff (2015) writes eloquently about moral injury when she says,

> As teachers who care, we open ourselves to… despair when our schools make decisions we can't influence and don't understand. We might begin to think of ourselves as failures or feel our work must not matter… I thought all of these things… I still sometimes do.

> (p. 50)

Another poignant demonstration of moral injury manifests through veteran public school educator Nancy Atwell, the winner of the first ever million-dollar Global Teacher Prize for education. Who, when excited reporters asked what advice she had for a student considering a career in teaching, said firmly, "I would discourage them unless they could find a job in a private school" (CNN, 2015). Oh yes, the injury is deep.

Avoidance, anxiety, and shame are traits of the morally injured and I am ashamed as I anxiously watch my strongBlackprofessor run away to avoid my pain. I am painfully aware that running away leaves those to whom I have dedicated my career to fight alone. In my avoidance, I have become all I tell my students not to be; but, if I remain a teacher educator, I am honestly unsure whether my continued presence supports or subverts those I teach. The decision to acquiesce to neoliberal reform – the very existence of an expectation that I should placidly implement "their" version of education – causes me to dry heave as I consider my permanent exit.

So Now What?

I would *so* like to conclude this chapter with a tender story about an epiphany that renews my commitment to public K-12 and teacher education, but I cannot. I am still struggling to answer key questions like: How should educators respond morally to the attempted systemic destruction of public education? What do we do with our feelings of moral injury? How can a strongBlackprofessor remain in a place of injury and still operate?

Because of my moral injury, I direct the CAS instead of teaching full-time. I know I am not in the right place; yet, I am bona fide confused about what my place should be. Soon, I must make a final decision about which identity will prevail, the "morally injured," the strongBlackteacher, or another, yet unidentified, identity who has navigated the travails of the other two.

Audre Lorde (1988) once opined that caring for one's self, "is not self-indulgent," and instead described self-care as "self-preservation" and "an act of political warfare." Thus, a final question important for my health and sanity, and to so many others suffering from our own special brand of PTSD, has become, how do those of us dedicated to the education of students of the global majority, yet injured by the onslaught of neoliberal education policy, engage in self-care?

Today, right or wrong, this story ends with my conflicted version of self-care. I told Louis not to teach because *I just did not want one more public school educator to have to feel what I feel.* I did not want to waste his excellence on a system that will do its best to drain him of all that he intends to do for the African American community. Today, the identity I embody is that of a strongBlackprofessor who has been morally injured and left to die. Thus, given the current neoliberal influence in public education, with my remaining breath I am bellowing the sentiments of stic man – *fuck* education.

At least theirs.

So sad.

Acknowledgments

The author wishes to thank Louis, a dynamic young man who *will* make a difference.

& Break my heart!

Note

1   *Students of the global majority* represents populations characterized as "minority," "at risk," "underserved," "non-White," "of Color," "urban," "low socioeconomic status" and "poor," in the U.S. – all terms that are used to mask the hegemony of European American populations and the numeric and political actuality of Black, Brown, and lower income people worldwide.

References

100 Black Men of Atlanta, (n.d.). Retrieved from http://100blackmen-atlanta.org

Ahlquist, R., Gorski, P., & Montaño, T. (2011). *Assault on Kids: How hyper-accountability, corporatization, deficit ideologies, and Ruby Payne are destroying our schools*. New York, NY: Peter Lang.

ARC. (2013). Regional Snapshot (white paper). Atlanta, GA, US: Atlanta Regional Commission.

Baker, D. (2012). Chicago school teachers give us all a lesson. Retrieved from http://www.aljazeera.com/indepth/opinion/2012/09/201291774248929713.html, September 17.

Bristol, T. J. (2015). Black male teachers: There aren't enough of them. In Strauss, V. *The Washington Post*: Answer Sheet (Blog), April 28. Retrieved December 10, 2015 from www.washingtonpost.com/news/answer-sheet/wp/2015/04/28/black-male-teachers-there-arent-enough-of-them/.

Brown, M. J. (2015). Opt Out – A student's response to edTPA. *What's The Idea?* Summer 2014–Summer 2015 *3*(4), 4.

CNN. (2015). 1 Million awarded to exceptional teacher. (Video). Retrieved January 22, 2016 from: www.youtube.com/watch?v=tR_qW6IuXv0, March 17.

Croft, C., Roberts, M. A., & Stenhouse, V. (2016). The perfect storm of education reform: High-stakes testing and teacher evaluation. *Social Justice: A Journal of Crime, Conflict and World Order, 42*(1), 70–92.

dead prez. (2000). They Schools. Produced by Hedrush & dead prez. *Let's Get Free*. Loud Records & Columbia Records, under distribution from Relativity Records.

DeGruy, J. L. (2005). *Post Traumatic Slave Syndrome: America's legacy of enduring injury and healing*. Portland, OR: Uptone Press.

Edelman, S., Jamieson, A., & Schram, J. (2015). Principal commits suicide amid Common Core test scandal. *New York Post*, July 26. Retrieved from http://nypost.com/2015/07/26/principal-commits-suicide-amid-common-core-test-scandal/

Gonzalez, D. (2016) A beloved Bronx teacher retires after a conflict with his principal. *The New York Times*, January 24. Retrieved from http://mobile.nytimes.com/2016/01/25/nyregion/a-beloved-bronx-teacher-retires-after-a-conflict-with-his-principal.html?referer=http://mobile.nytimes.com/2016/01/27/opinion/a-teacher-disillusioned.html?emc=eta1&referer=

Grant, C., Brown, K. D., & Brown, A. L. (2016). *Black Intellectual Thought in Education*. New York, NY: Routledge.

Holzman, M. (2010). *Yes We Can: The Schott 50 state report on public education and Black males*. Cambridge, MA: The Schott Foundation.

Hursh, D. W. (2016). *The End of Public Schools: The corporate reform agenda to privatize education*. New York, NY: Routledge.

Ladson-Billings, G. (2005). *Beyond the Big House: African American teachers on teacher education.* New York, NY: Teacher's College Press.

Layton, L. (2015). Wanted in New York City: A thousand Black, Latino, and Asian male teachers. *The Washington Post.* Retrieved from www.washingtonpost.com/local/education/wanted-in-new-york-city-a-thousand-black-latino-and-asian-male-teachers/2015/12/11/a8cc0f52-9f7f-11e5-a3c5-c77f2cc5a43c_story.html

Litz, B. T., Stein, N., Delaney, E., Lebowitz, L., Nash, W. P., Silva, C., & Maguen, S. (2009). Moral injury and moral repair in war veterans: A preliminary model and intervention strategy. *Clinical Psychology Review, 29,* 695–706.

Lorde, A. (1988). *A Burst of Light: Essays.* Ann Arbor, MI: Firebrand Books.

Madeloni, B., & Gorlewski, J. (2013). Wrong answer to the wrong question: Why we need critical teacher education, not standardization. *Rethinking Schools, 27*(4), 16–21.

Moguldom Media Group (2014). *72%.* Retrieved from http://moguldomstudios.com/films/72/?utm_source=madamenoire&utm_medium=advertorial&utm_content=&utm_campaign=72

Morgan, J. (1999). *When Chickenheads Come Home to Roost: My life as a hip hop feminist.* New York, NY: Simon and Schuster.

National Center for Education Statistics (NCES) (2016). The Condition of Education. Retrieved from http://nces.ed.gov/programs/coe/indicator_cge.asp

National Center for Fair and Open Testing (2010). Racial justice and standardized educational testing. Retrieved from www.fairtest.org/sites/default/files/racial_justice_and_testing_12-10.pdf

Noguera, P. (2009). *The trouble with Black boys…and Other Reflections on Race, Equity and the Future of Public Education.* San Francisco, CA: Jossey-Bass.

Porosoff, L. (2015). Healing from moral injury. *Teaching Tolerance, Fall 2015,* 49–51.

Ravitch, D. (2010). *The Death and Life of the Great American School System: How testing and choice are undermining education.* New York, NY: Basic Books.

Rivera, S. (2013). Growing losses: List of teachers who have publicly resigned. *Teacher Under Construction* (Blog). Retrieved from http://teacherunderconstruction.com/2012/11/22/list-of-2012-student-protests-regarding-education-in-the-u-s/

Roberts, M. A. (2015). The testing industrial complex: Incarcerating education since 2001. In M. Abendroth, & B. Porfilio (Eds.). *School against Neoliberal Rule: Educational fronts for local and global justice: A reader.* Charlotte, NC: Information Age Publishing.

USDOE Office for Civil Rights (2014, March). Civil rights data collection: Data snapshot (school discipline). Retrieved from http://ocrdata.ed.gov/Downloads/CRDC-School-Discipline-Snapshot.pdf

Yancy, G., & hooks, b. (2015, December 10). bell hooks: Buddhism, the beats and loving Blackness. *The New York Times Opinionator.* (Blog). Retrieved from http://opinionator.blogs.nytimes.com/2015/12/10/bell-hooks-buddhism-the-beats-and-loving-blackness/?_r=0

Part II
Navigating Whiteness

6 Privileging the Pragmatic

Interrogating Stance in Teacher Preparation

Alison G. Dover

As a White teacher educator, I spend a lot of time talking about race. I sit in predominantly White faculty meetings where I talk to other White teacher educators about recruiting and retaining a diverse pool of teacher candidates. We disaggregate data from the growing number of tests required for teacher licensure, and write reports forecasting the disparate impact of those tests on candidates of Color. We critique the whiteness implicit in the literary canon, P-12 curriculum, success of the testing industry, and our own requirements. We recognize that whiteness is overwhelming, in our field, our communities, our students, and ourselves. We know it, and we talk about it. But we never seem to know what to do. *And this is why we research a large gap.*

This is not a new statement, nor is it especially controversial. Much has been written about White inaction on critical issues of institutional racism, both within and beyond the academy (e.g. Gorski, 2015; Hayes & Fasching-Varner, 2015; Picower & Mayorga, 2015). My White colleagues and I talk about the "pipeline problem" but, despite our supposed best intentions, over and over again, our field fails to effectively recruit or retain candidates of Color. Our classrooms, our faculty meetings, our graduation ceremonies are predominantly White, even in institutions – like my own – that serve a racially, ethnically, and linguistically diverse student body. There is a problem with whiteness in teacher education. And White teacher educators are good at *talking* about it.

For me, talking about whiteness is easy. Doing so in ways that do not privilege White needs, priorities, and narratives is harder. I have yet to meet a White teacher educator who does not have a secret shady story about a time when our whiteness got in the way – not our White race, but our White mindset – and prevented us from asking the question or doing the analysis or taking the action we should have. We need to acknowledge this: *yes* privilege is seductive, and we get sucked in all the time. *I* get sucked in all the time. But, I am still grappling with public racial reflection: writing about the evolution of my whiteness feels both self-indulgent and revealing. I do not particularly want to trade on the experiences that shaped my lens, nor do I identify with the "scholarship" of whiteness. I would prefer to be a voyeur, devouring the narratives of others without risking my own. Writing this chapter is uncomfortable; but the ability to opt out of discomfort is part of my privilege. As a White teacher educator, I'm rarely held accountable for the ways my own identity and stance inform my work.

This is me: I am a White, working class, queer femme, a first generation college graduate and a teacher educator. I am also an imposter. As was the case for other ethnic, working class Whites, racist lending and housing policies bought my parents access to a wealthy White neighborhood. The town I grew up in was more than 98% White, had a median income twice the national average and was known for stellar K–12 schools. While my family worked to stretch the food budget, one of the kids at school had a *three lane bowling alley* in her basement. I always felt "different," but White privilege paved my way. My schools had abundant resources, opportunities for enrichment, and proactive guidance counselors. Collectively, these led to admission at, and a scholarship for, an elite private university. I was the poor kid there too, but I learned to (mostly) pass. There were moments of terrible, shameful, disconnect: times I went hungry, was denied access, or straddled the line between humbled and humiliated. But I was there, and it launched me.

I do not mean to sound trite. Socialization by fire is painful, and twenty years later, I still bear scars. Over time, I have learned to spin a revisionist narrative about my college experience: it was character-building, provided insight into the experiences of marginalized students, and prepared me to help others navigate hostile systems. This creative retelling usually works, and I am able to convince myself that I gained more than the sheer privilege of passing.

And what a privilege it is. When White, middle class educational gatekeepers hear me talk they assume I came from wealth; invariably, many presume I am *just like them*. They make reference to our (fictional) shared worldview, one shaped by similar childhood experiences, adolescent values, and social networks. Being an imposter gets me a seat at the table, an invitation to join the conversation, despite having as much in common with the euphemistic "those kids" who are subjects of education policy as with the adults who write, debate, enforce, and profit from it. I do not say this to deny or distance myself from my whiteness, but to complicate it: part of my privilege is the access that comes with being read as someone I am (was) not.

I could tell a similar story through the lens of gender and queerness. As a queer femme, not passing as straight requires effort: it is amazing what people read into a pair of heels. Over the years, I have at times passed strategically, passed inadvertently, and refused to pass at all. It is the privilege of an imposter: I get to narrate my own identity, choosing what to reveal, to whom, and under what circumstances. In more reflective moments, I pay attention to the subtle evolution toward invisibility: age and class privilege have muted my high femme flamboyance, the margins of queer identity have shifted, and my life appears quite straight. I have a husband and two kids. We shop organic and live in the suburbs. Heteronormativity fuels the illusion, and I fly under the radar all the time.

As a justice oriented high school teacher, being an imposter served me well. Rather than viewing my "non-traditional" approach as a threat, my White, male principal indulged my activist curriculum. After all, I looked like him, got my lesson plans in on time, and had high pass rates on the mandated tests (something we both, at the time, considered a valid indicator of teacher effectiveness). Like many imposters, I knew how to work the system: I code switched with fluency, met the requirements, smiled at administrators, and agitated behind the scenes. My whiteness and femininity enabled me to be strategically covert.

I have gotten so good at appearing compliant that I sometimes catch myself forgetting my own story, seduced by the fictions of others' assumptions and the privileges they carry. Until the moment when I say too much and mention working an assembly line, or skipping school to get high, or just why my heart broke when Leslie Feinberg died. I watch eyebrows go up and am reminded of how easy it is to be swept up by the tide of privilege. Unlike my students, my colleagues, my community, who do not have the privileges of passing, I have the choice to opt out, anytime I like.

These questions of privilege and stance came up recently during a conversation with a fellow White, justice oriented colleague, as we debated how to best prepare teacher candidates for the latest round of neoliberal policy assaults in our state. My colleague, who holds professional and economic privilege, encourages students to – at least temporarily – view the mandates as irrelevant. During a visit to my class on teaching for social justice, he actually told my students to "fuck the standards," something I cannot imagine ever saying while teaching a class. There was a pause. Several students smiled; a few squirmed. His point was to challenge candidates to focus on first developing a progressive, student-centered philosophy; they could deal with the standards, methods, and mandates later. It is a powerful approach, and I happen to agree: our collective emphasis on standards is limiting, de-professionalizing, and antithetical to transformative change. His suggestion, however, was also predicated on the assumption that our candidates, many of whom are first generation college attendees and graduates of the urban classrooms in which they hope to teach, will flourish despite the hostile regulatory climate.

I would like to believe that, but struggle to shake my pragmatic emphasis on meeting the mandates first. My colleague's perspective reflects a freedom I did not have. As an imposter, I am trained to figure out the rules before I navigate the world, and carry this pragmatism into the classroom. This approach appeals to my students: they, too, have learned to prioritize the practical. They do not believe doors will open easily to them, and are well trained to respect institutional power. They appreciate my emphasis on code switching, deconstructing the mandates, and preparing to teach effectively within and despite broken systems. However, collective vision of just schooling is defined in response to a neoliberal, corporate, and exploitative educational landscape (Gorlewski, Porfilio, & Gorlewski, 2011; Nichols &

Berliner, 2007). My colleague made me wonder: who am I serving by teaching the tactics of subversion rather than resistance?

This question resonates as I consider the current onslaught of accountability mandates in teacher education, such as the rapid institutionalization of high-stakes, standardized teacher performance assessments (TPAs). Touted as a response to the (manufactured) crisis of teacher quality, TPAs are sweeping the nation. In just three years, one such assessment, edTPA, has been rolled out in 700 educator preparation programs across 38 states (AACTE, n.d.). As is the case of other neoliberal education reforms, edTPA has been criticized for better serving corporate bottom lines than teacher candidates: justice oriented scholars challenge its design, validity, cost, implementation, impact, and blatant disregard for contextually relevant practice (Dover & Schultz, 2016; Jordan & Hawley, 2016; Madeloni, 2015). In the overwhelmingly White field of teaching and teacher education, critiques like these are accepted as the norm.

Ironically, some advocates argue that edTPA could encourage preparation programs to engage issues of cultural relevance (Lynn, 2014). After all, there is *one* question for which a passing score requires candidates to "justif[y] why learning tasks (or their adaptations) are appropriate using examples of students' prior academic learning OR personal, cultural, or community assets" (SCALE, 2015, p. 16, emphasis in original). I suppose it is possible that that question might spark conversation within institutions that have historically marginalized culturally responsive practices. But, it is a bit of a stretch. There are also published examples of how teacher candidates can enact justice oriented curriculum within and despite the confines of edTPA's structure (e.g. Dover & Pozdol, 2016). As a field, we are again trying to find ways to be subversive, to promote justice in a hostile system. At heart, though, there is no doubt that high-cost, high-stakes, standardized teacher evaluation systems will privilege certain (White, middle and upper class) candidates teaching in certain (White, normative, prescriptive) ways in certain (White, suburban, wealthy) schools. Ultimately, edTPA is yet another racist education policy, designed to colonize teaching and learning (Tuck & Gorlewski, 2016).

But in faculty meetings, our fervor is too often focused on the implications for our own curriculum and programming, not the greater assault it represents. In recent months, I have spent countless hours discussing how to prepare candidates for the "new reality" and ourselves for the inevitable impact on enrollment. We hold trainings for faculty supervisors, school-based partners, and teacher candidates. We strategize about how to help our candidates demonstrate fluency in the types of academic language privileged by edTPA. We write letters, op-eds, blog posts, journal articles, and tweets. Far too many of us, myself included, are doing what teacher educators do well. We are talking about "the problem," as if the racial implications of teacher education policy are a topic for academic inquiry rather than part of a hydra-headed agenda that perpetuates the systemic oppression of children and communities of Color in the United States (Picower & Mayorga, 2015).

I do not mean to suggest that my colleagues and I do not have an activist stance; many of us do. That stance led us to this particular college of education, in a public Hispanic Serving Institution that prepares first generation, justice oriented, community teachers. Many of us are first generation academics ourselves, with more in common with our candidates – and their future students – than stereotypes about academia might suggest. In any one of those meetings I referenced, there are people who have been on many sides of the prism of privilege.

Behind closed doors, my colleagues and I share the messy bits of our own stories, talk about how our privileges protected us, or failed to protect us, and remember the intense, overwhelming anger and shame that comes when you are at the mercy of an unjust system. We acknowledge the racial double standards illustrated by hashtags like #CrimingWhileWhite and #AliveWhileBlack. Behind closed doors, we grapple with the implications of wealth or whiteness, and wonder how to reconcile our justice work with the decision to move out of the city, to send our children to schools that are "safe, liberal, and academic, but still really diverse." We describe the tensions of walking the tightrope between where we came from and where we stand today. Behind closed doors, many White teacher educators are fierce about issues of justice in our neighborhoods, involved in community organizing, and vocal in our critique of local and national education policy.

So why, when crafting institutional guidelines and responding to state mandates, do we so often leave that urgency at the door? We bemoan the onslaught of neoliberal reform and critique the rhetoric of choice. But we also push back on institutional directives that curtail our academic freedom more vehemently than those that perpetuate the inequities we purport to oppose. Perhaps it is a function of our privilege. Or perhaps we have been lulled into complicity by a constellation of ever-changing mandates that interrupt the momentum of our movements, tempting us to focus on the heads of the hydra rather than the overarching politics at play.

There are many White teacher educators who use their scholarly platform to fight for racial justice in education. I like to consider myself one of them. However, I question the ways that our version of activist scholarship functions as yet another professionally sanctioned opportunity to *talk*. In his provocative comparison of the radical vision of the Black Lives Matter movement and the polite, "respectable" discourse of educational research, Dumas (2016) challenges scholars to consider how antiblackness influences our collective reluctance to use disruptive activism to derail unjust policy. He argues that in the current political and educational climate, "simply writing another 'critical' book or article, or even sitting on another diversity commission, is not enough," that it is time for academics to stop talking and begin to "shut shit down" (p. 9). This parsing of activist scholarship and activist action strikes me as somewhere my own pragmatic compliance continues to get in the way.

As I write this, I must admit that my reflection came in the context of an attack on *my* interests. I have spent the several last years writing, talking, and teaching about issues of social, racial, and educational activism and justice. But not shutting shit down. In 2016, though, things changed. The state in which I lived and worked (Illinois) failed to pass a state budget, withholding funding from institutions of public higher education for more than ten months. When funds came through, they were for just 30% of the previous year's budget. Tens of thousands of students were denied need-based scholarships, and thousands of faculty and staff were furloughed or laid off. This crisis destabilized communities and disproportionately affected poor people and people of Color: Chicago State University, a predominantly Black university, was forced to shorten their semester and lay off more than a third of their workforce. Illinois' "pro-business" governor is unapologetically dismantling public higher education, and we have been unable to stop him.

This is an outrage. It is right that I am outraged. However, this is not the first policy assault on poor people and people of Color since I moved to Illinois. Racial and educational injustice in Chicago has a long, vicious history. It is just the first time that *I* was in the streets, the first time *I* was forced to contemplate what it means to shut shit down. That is an unlovely admission: my privilege led me to talk about issues that require action. I have always seen my role as one of subversive pragmatism, enacting justice within and despite hostile systems. I question, now, who this strategy was actually serving. Have I become so good at being an imposter that I stopped paying attention to whom I am actually accountable?

Our field is in crisis and as teacher educators we must let our urgency move us. *I* must let *my* urgency move *me*. And so I am taking the advice I have long given candidates: I will teach – and act – to my conscience, ask what really matters, and take action to elicit change. When you see me in the future, ask me not only what I have written and what I have said, but how I have listened and what I have done. I will not be passing for compliant any more.

References

American Association of Colleges of Teacher Education (AACTE). (n.d.) edTPA Participation Map. Retrieved from http://edtpa.aacte.org/state-policy.

Dover, A. G., & Pozdol, T. (2016). Teaching good kids in a m.a.a.d. world: Using hip-hop to reflect, reframe, and respond to complex realities. *English Journal, 105*(4), 45–50.

Dover, A.G., & Schultz, B. D. (2016). Troubling the edTPA: Illusions of objectivity and rigor. *The Educational Forum, 80*(1), 95–106.

Dumas, M. J. (2016). Shutting Ish Down: Black lives matter as a challenge to the field of education. *Division B Newsletter: Black Lives Matter*. Washington, DC: AERA.

Gorlewski, J., Porfilio, B., & Gorlewski, D. (Eds.). (2011). *Using Standards and High-Stakes Testing for Students: Exploiting power with critical pedagogy*. New York, NY: Peter Lang.

Gorski, P. (2015). Ferguson and the violence of 'it's-all-about-me' White liberalism. In K. Fasching-Varner et al. (Eds.), *The Assault on Communities of Color: Exploring the realities of race-based violence* (pp. 33–37). New York, NY: Rowman & Littlefield.

Hayes, C. & Fasching-Varner, K. (2015). Racism 2.0 and the death of social and cultural foundations of education: A critical conversation. *The Journal of Educational Foundations, 28*, 103–119.

Jordan, A. W., & Hawley, T. (2016). By the elite, for the vulnerable: The edTPA, academic oppression, and the battle to define good teaching. *Teachers College Record*, February 15. Retrieved from www.tcrecord.org/content. asp?contentid=1946

Lynn, M. (2014). Making culturally relevant pedagogy relevant to aspiring teachers. *Diverse Issues in Higher Education*, March 19. Retrieved from http://diverseeducation.com/article/61280/

Madeloni, B. (2015). edTPA: Doubling down on Whiteness in teacher education. In B. Picower & E. Mayorga (Eds.), *What's Race Got to Do with It? How current school reform policy maintains racial and economic inequality* (pp. 167–182). New York, NY: Peter Lang.

Nichols, S. L., & Berliner, D. C. (2007). *Collateral Damage: How high-stakes testing corrupts America's schools*. Cambridge, MA: Harvard Education Press.

Picower, B., & Mayorga, E. (2015). *What's Race Got to Do with It? How current school reform policy maintains racial and economic inequality*. New York, NY: Peter Lang.

Stanford Center for Assessment, Learning, and Equity (SCALE). (2015). *edTPA Secondary English Language Arts Assessment Handbook: September 2015*. Stanford, CA: Author.

Tuck, E., & Gorlewski, J. A. (2016). Racist ordering, settler colonialism, and edTPA: A participatory policy analysis. *Journal of Educational Policy, 30*(1), 197–217.

7 "Written All Over My Face"

A Black Man's Toll of Teaching White Students about Racism

Daren Graves

The Toll the Work has Taken

It was a Monday morning in November. I started my normal routine before I headed to work. I finished brushing my teeth and began to rinse my mouth out. As I attempted to swirl the water inside my mouth, half of the water sprayed outside of the right side of my mouth. After I thought I had just made a silly mistake, I tried again, and it happened again. It very soon became clear to me that the right side of my face was becoming paralyzed. As I stood and looked at myself in the mirror, I froze. "I'm having a stroke," I thought. I immediately told my wife what was happening to me and we headed off to the hospital. In the car, I remember thinking, "Wow, I'm having a stroke. What if this is it for me?" I was 36 years old at the time. But I kept feeling quite lucid, just paralyzed on the right side of my face. After some tests from my doctor, the diagnosis came back.

> "Bell's Palsy. BP," he said.
> "OK. How do we fix it?" I asked.
> The doctor replied, "Well, that's complicated… It's idiopathic."
> "Idiopathic?" I wondered aloud.
> "Yes it means we don't know what the cause is. It's not likely swelling around the facial nerve. Some folks think it might be caused by a virus, or even stress. Have you been stressed lately?" the doctor explained.
> "How long will it last?" I asked desperately.
> The doctor replied, "Hard to tell. Some people, it goes away in a week. For most, six to eight weeks. For some six months to a year. And for a very few it never goes away, but that's usually for folks older than you."

The thought of weeks, months, or years felt excruciatingly long to me in that moment. For seven weeks I was unable to control the muscles on the right side of my face. And while the fact that I would have to do my job as a professor without the function of half of my face would prove to be daunting, my doctor's question about stress and what I was about to experience for the foreseeable future brought deeper issues to the forefront of my consciousness.

"Have You Been Stressed Lately?" Navigating Whiteness in Courses about Racism

My doctor's question about my stress haunted me as I prepared to cope with teaching classes without the use of half of my face. My smile now looked like a smirk. My normal gaze now made me look disinterested and unsympathetic. As I reflected on how I would have to perform my duties in the classroom as I endured the symptoms of BP, the ways in which my performance as a teacher were dictated by my race-gendered intersectional identity became more clear and disturbing to me than on previous reflection. Patton and Catching (2009) and McGowan's (2000) research illuminates how White students challenged African American faculty members' authority in the classroom and/or expertise in their academic fields. These experiences often led to negative evaluations of African American faculty (Patton & Catching, 2009) by their students. As a teacher educator, an assistant professor at one institution and as an adjunct professor at another, decisions about my tenure and/or retention heavily relied on the feedback I received from students on course evaluations. Additionally, the courses I teach require students to interrogate how racism operates in the field of education. Mirroring the racial and gendered composition of the field of teaching in the U.S., the majority of my students are White women. I experienced many of the "tools of Whiteness" that Picower (2009) outlines where White teacher candidates employ rhetorical and ideological tools to resist against meaningfully reflecting on their teaching practices and ideologies as they intersect with race.

For example, White students have expressed that I, or the course material, made them feel guilty as they learned about racism or unearned White privilege. Other students have expressed (explicitly and implicitly) that racism is a remnant of the past that does not warrant interrogation because they do not see themselves or their colleagues as engaging in racism in contemporary contexts. And while I never was explicitly told to not teach about racism, my colleagues did give me advice that I needed to figure out ways to improve the students' evaluations of these courses to improve my chances of earning tenure. The pressure I faced to improve students' course evaluations compelled me to suppress the anxiety I felt before classes.

Because the institution that I was trying to earn tenure at placed so much value on the feedback in the course evaluations, I was worried that students would evaluate me or the course poorly. My fears were realized when I received comments like "The material is repetitive…" or relatively lower rankings on questions asking students to evaluate the utility of the course. I felt indignation toward my students who resisted my personal and professional expertise by implicitly and explicitly indicating that they felt the subject material was not important to their learning and growth as educators. I would often feel shame at the end of classes for allowing students' resistance to go somewhat unchallenged because of my fear of the negative implications of being poorly evaluated. "What kind of example am I setting as a teacher educator around deconstructing racism, if I can't even name racism or resistance to learn about it in my own classroom?" I thought.

In essence, my White students and I co-constructed a teaching persona that allowed me to teach my material while accommodating their anxieties and fears about learning about racism from a Black man. As a co-author of the article written by Truong, Graves, and Keene (2014), I spoke about the ways I developed a consciousness about my tone as I taught about racism, out of fear that my presentation as a Black man might cause my White students to misconstrue my sarcasm or attempts at comedy for anger or lack of intellectual capability.

One particular experience with a White student illuminated how the persona we had co-constructed made me question the ways it authentically represented my experiences as a Black man, and expertise as a scholar. During a break in a class where I was teaching preservice students about racism, a White student asked me a few questions about some of the material we had just learned. Earlier in the class, I shared ways in which I had experienced mundane and exceptional forms of racism in my daily life. The student asked me, "How often does that happen to you?" Before it became clear that she was asking me about how often I endure forms of racism, I looked at her with a confused expression because I wasn't sure what the "that" referred to. The fact that my response of "All the time" seemed to surprise her left me wondering how much she had absorbed from my lessons about the pervasiveness of racism. Her next question cut very deep and had me questioning even further. "Oh… How do you deal with it so well?"

The student's very genuine question left me further in doubt as to whether my messages about the commonness of racism and the ways we get socialized into reproducing it as a system was getting through. It also made me wonder what type of disposition I was displaying as a Black man teaching mainly White women about race. Having endured racism in many forms on a daily basis, I would never characterize the way I was "dealing with it" as "well." I could bear witness to the pain that I felt and how subdued I was as I navigated racism in society. I construed the student's comment and its tone to connote that I seemed unaffected by racism. It made me think more critically about how I presented in my teaching as I consciously attended to the comfort of the White women in my class.

The emotional violence I experienced was the result of both the anxiety I faced as I became hyper-aware of the ways students' resistance could sink my professional career, as well as the anger I felt as a result of the indignities I faced as my own lived experiences and expertise were devalued by my students. My anticipation of the emotional violence brought on further anxiety, which led to a variety of mild physical symptoms (e.g., nausea, high blood pressure) that I had to overcome to teach my classes effectively. These physical symptoms culminated with the aforementioned BP in the year leading up to my tenure review. While it is impossible to say that my attempts to cope with the racism I faced from my students were the direct cause of my BP, my health providers hypothesized that my condition was at least exacerbated (if not caused) by coping with severe stress. I had no doubt at the time the anxiety I faced coping with and responding to the racism I faced in the classroom was at the forefront of feeding into my experiences of stress. How ironic that my attempts to obscure the ways that anxiety and stress were taking their emotional and physical toll on me resulted in a condition where my stress and anxiety were literally written all over my face.

The emotional and physical toll that I endure(d) to navigate racism inside and outside of the classroom is very likely exacting detrimental physical and emotional effects on me (McGee & Stovall, 2015). It was this fact that made the "How do you deal with it so well?" question feel so profoundly concerning. I was not dealing with racism "well" and the fact that the student might conceive of me (or anyone) in that way spoke to ways in which I needed to improve how I teach my students about racism. Both for the sake of my professional development and for my health, I need my students (especially the White ones) to better understand the ways that they can and do reinforce racism inside the classroom, while also keeping them actively engaged in learning and focused on being critically reflective participants. The cognitive dissonance I experienced in that moment, the indignities I faced as White students resisted learning, and how these students misunderstood the ways racism operated inside and outside of the classroom, compelled me to fine tune how I teach about how racism operates as a system in the contemporary context.

"No Safe Zone. No End Zone" – Tools for Teaching White Teachers about Racism

My tenure depended heavily on my White students' evaluations of my courses, and the more comfortable my students were, the more likely I would receive positive evaluations. In this regard, I developed some teaching tools in the context of the emotional violence I faced and absorbed as many White students actively/passively resisted meaningful learning in my classes.

While I do not find it productive to promise "safe spaces" in my courses about racism, I do have an interest in fostering a classroom community where all students can meaningfully participate and learn. In the most basic principles of cognitive development theory (Piaget, 1972; Vygotsky, 1978), we know that meaningful learning requires experiencing some level of discomfort. When it comes to learning about unearned privilege, discriminatory systems, and oppression, this principle holds true even more so. Learning about racism, whether through peer reviewed texts, or by reflecting on the racialized lived experiences shared by their classmates, is an exercise in understanding the way that racism produces a lack of safety on systematic and hegemonic levels. To promise or to even hope to achieve "safety" in our classrooms seems counterproductive in this regard. My commitment to creating a "safe space" also presumes that I, as the Black male professor, am free of reinforcing racism or other oppressive systems such as sexism or homophobia in the classroom (hooks, 1994). Just because one teaches and researches about racism, or just because one might be a person of Color, does not mean that one cannot perpetuate racism inside or outside of classrooms.

This speaks to a "no end zone" principle that I introduce to my students early in classes. Research has shown that among the many reasons why White people express why they find it difficult to learn about racism in classroom settings stems from a sense of feeling shame or guilt about being White and a feeling that the teacher/facilitator is talking down to them or patronizing them (Picower, 2009). Some White students whose trust I earned have felt comfortable telling me that it can be hard as a White student learning about racism from a Black person. When I have probed further about why the learning might be more difficult coming from a Black teacher, my students expressed they felt like I had some racialized lived experiences that gave me a level of expertise and perspective on issues of racism that they could never achieve as White folks.

I came to understand that students should learn early on that there is no threshold of knowledge that then makes you racism-free. Rather, because race itself is such a dynamic construct (Delgado & Stefancic, 2012), it requires one to be nimble and constantly reflective to effectively understand how racism is operating at any given time. If anything sets apart the teacher from the person less educated about race, it is the fact that the teacher may be engaged in a more consistent critically reflective process about issues of race and racism. In other words, instead of conceiving of their professor as having reached the threshold of knowledge it takes to reach the "Racism-Free End Zone," they should seek to emulate the way the professor reflects on the ways they struggle in not reproducing oppression both inside and outside the classroom. At the same time, I also teach that while we can all condone or challenge institutional racism, our racial positionality influences the nature of, and implications for, how this can happen. This means that my White students also need to come to understand that whether and how they engage in reproducing oppression is different for them relative to me because of the different levels and forms of power and privilege we are conferred on the basis of race.

Conclusion

The disproportionate energy and focus on the comfort of my White students as they interrogate racism can be construed as reinforcing racism in these classroom spaces. Given that I employ critical analysis of race in my research and teaching, I am not surprised racism reproduces itself inside our classroom spaces. The fact that racism is to be expected in classroom spaces does not necessarily meaningfully mitigate the deleterious effects it has on my emotional or physical health. Administrators and committees on Promotion and Tenure need to understand that White students may express their dissonance and discomfort through course evaluations (Deo, 2015; Evans-Winters & Twyman Hoff, 2011), and to look at course evaluations in these situations accordingly as they evaluate the professional development of the faculty teaching these courses. These administrators and committees should also be more educated about effective pedagogies for how to teach about racism, and how these pedagogies might result in students experiencing dissonance or discomfort.

More importantly, the field of teacher education needs to be reformed to reflect the notion that studying issues of racism in education is an essential part of becoming a highly qualified teacher. As it stands right now, the study of racism in education is often relegated to elective courses or given superficial coverage in required courses. This sends the message that studying issues of racism in education is optional or marginal relative to other topics in the field of teacher education, and therefore informs or validates the behaviors of White students who resist learning about racism in the realm of education. Rendering the study of racism as marginal or optional also belies both the expertise of teachers of Color and a growing and profound body of research that shows the many ways that racism impacts the learning and teaching process.

References

Delgado, R., & Stefancic, J. (2012). *Critical Race Theory. [electronic resource]: An introduction.* New York, NY: New York University Press.

Deo, M. E. (2015). A better tenure battle: Fighting bias in teaching evaluations. *Columbia Journal of Gender and Law, 31*(1), 7–43.

Evans-Winters, V. E., & Twyman Hoff, P. (2011). The aesthetics of white racism in pre-service teacher education: A critical race theory perspective. *Race, Ethnicity and Education, 14*(4), 461.

hooks, b. (1994). *Teaching to Transgress: Education as the practice of freedom.* New York, NY: Routledge.

McGee, E. O., & Stovall, D. (2015). Reimagining critical race theory in education: Mental health, healing, and the pathway to liberatory praxis. *Educational Theory, 65*, 491–511.

McGowan, J. M. (2000). Multicultural teaching: African American faculty classroom teaching experiences in predominantly White colleges and universities. *Multicultural Education, 8*(2), 19–22.

Patton, L. D., & Catching, C. (2009). Teaching while Black: Narratives of African American student affairs faculty. *International Journal of Qualitative Studies, 22*(6), 713–728.

Piaget, J. (1972). *The Psychology of the Child.* New York, NY: Basic Books.

Picower, B. (2009). The unexamined whiteness of teaching: How white teachers maintain and enact dominant racial ideologies. *Race, Ethnicity and Education, 12*(2), 197–215.

Truong, K. A., Graves, D., & Keene, A. J. (2014). Faculty of color teaching critical race theory at a PWI: An autoethnography. *Journal of Critical Thought and Praxis, 3*(2). Retrieved from http://lib.dr.iastate.edu/jctp/vol3/iss2/4

Vygotsky, L. S. (1978). *Mind in Society: The development of higher psychological processes.* Cambridge, MA: Harvard University Press.

8 "No, Really... Call Me Crazy"

Reclaiming Identity through Vulnerability in Teacher Education

Jillian Carter Ford

I am a Black/White biracial queer woman with mental illness and a disposition for social justice. I am also a teacher educator at a large southern regional comprehensive university in a county that – until recently – was a notorious bastion of White evangelical conservatism. As a way to address the dangerous silences around mental illness, I decided to come out as "crazy" to my preservice teacher education students beginning fall 2014, my fourth year as an assistant professor. I continue to do so for three main reasons. First, claiming crazy helps me introduce the power of words and word reclamation. Second, it serves to illustrate one of my many identities that shape my perspectives: a central concept I intend for my students to learn. Third, it demonstrates both a level of vulnerability (Dimitriadis, Cole, & Costello, 2009) necessary for transformative education (Friere, 1970) and an invitation for others to share their mental health experiences. In order to deconstruct social taboos, we must break our silences (Lorde, 1984).

In this chapter, I illustrate factors that contributed to paralyzing depressive episodes and strategies I employed to heal. I reflect on how my mental and emotional rollercoaster was affected by and affected my work as a teacher educator.

Growing Up Raced and Classed

As a fifth-grader in the late 1980s, I was selected to be an inaugural chorus member for a newly formed children's music group in New York. Our music was intended to inspire children to respect one another across difference, see value in independence, cherish our elders, and other similar liberal values. All of our music aligned perfectly with my beliefs, which by age 10 were already deeply rooted: of course differently abled people should be included; humanity is a rainbow, and curiosity a virtue. We celebrated diversity, and cheerfully encouraged others to join the fun.

Like many kids with one White parent and one Black parent who came of age before the twenty-first century, my parents explained to my siblings and me that we were Black kids with light brown skin. We know this emerged from the insidious laws upon which this country was built: that one drop of

Black blood made one Black. Of course this ensured the incentive of increased wealth for White slave masters' rape of Black women. Still I was comforted by the simplicity of being grouped within a category I knew and understood. It was not until fifth grade, by which point I had recognized the patterns in "ability" grouping in school, that I began to feel different from my other Black friends. By the time I reached high school I identified more as biracial; a label I used and still use interchangeably or in conjunction with Black.

I am the youngest of three children born into an upper middle class family in a small college town in largely rural upstate New York. Our father was an Ivy League university professor and our mother an administrator at the same school, which gave my siblings and me incredible access to books, technology, speakers, performances, and international travel throughout our childhood. By the end of elementary school, I was already hyper-aware that both race and class influenced academic grouping in schools: I was routinely separated from most of my Black and low income White friends, of which I had many.

The Making of Crazy

In *The Wretched of the Earth*, Fanon (1963) reflected on and wrote about the Algerian independence struggle, including colonialism's role in individual and collective manifestations of mental illness. As a psychiatrist, Fanon and his medical colleagues published papers discussing the "difficulty of 'curing' a colonized subject correctly" (Fanon, 1963, p. 182). To illustrate his point, Fanon described the common recurrence of a "psychotic reaction" wherein "priority [was] given to the situation that triggered the disorder" (p. 183). The "situation" to which he referred was both the oppression inherent to colonial rule and the bloody anticolonial struggle.

It is not my intention to imply that traumatic experiences in my life have been remotely similar to anyone who lived through war. Instead, I wish to lift the general concept that psychiatric diagnoses can be directly related to the state-mandated rules of society. Perhaps my own educational experiences as a queer Black girl in U.S. public schools – along with my efforts as an adult to improve educational quality for marginalized youth – had played a role in my own battles with mental illness. It was freeing to consider a source outside genetics; it flipped my shame into honor. Interesting!

In his introduction to Friere's seminal *Pedagogy of the Oppressed*, Macedo (2000) described a paradox that traps many of us constrained by colonial systems. Macedo explains that the book fueled his own "inner strength to begin the arduous process of transcending a colonial existence that is almost culturally schizophrenic: being present and yet not visible, being visible and yet not present" (p. 11). Laymon (2013) described the phenomenon this way in his collected essays titled *How to Slowly Kill Yourself and Others in America*:

> *The worst of white folks*… wasn't some gang of rabid white people in crisp pillowcases and shaved heads. *The worst of white folks* was a pathetic,

powerful "it." It conveniently forgot that it came to this country on a boat, then reacted violently when anything or anyone suggested it share … It was all at once crazy-making and quick to violently discipline us for acting crazy.

(p. 28)

Grappling with Fanon's, Macedo's, and Laymon's theories allowed me to step out of the torments and paralysis of my own battles with depression. Western psychiatry rests in part on the understanding that mental illness is individual and chemically-inherent. The possibility that mental illness could result from the conditions in an oppressive state allowed me to surface from isolation. In asserting my craziness, I was reminded of the power that accompanies reclaiming words meant to shame. This renders powerless those people and forces that seek to extinguish my light.

Crazy 101: Graduate School

Although my difficulties manifested in physical ways, I certainly experienced them within materially privileged contexts wherein I had actual access to virtually every resource one could imagine. This produced a level of guilt that cycled nastily with the tangible ways in which universities marginalize people of Color and do little to support mental wellness.

When I entered graduate school as a student, the university's racial climate was already strained. Founded in 1836 in Georgia, the school was built by enslaved Black people and run by wealthy slave owners. My time in graduate school was punctuated by racist incidents common in many predominantly White institutions. The percentage of Black faculty and students was very low, yet Black employees filled the majority of low wage service jobs. On more than one occasion, White students donned Blackface for Halloween, with no detectable consequences. The university administration announced it was closing several departments (including educational studies, where I was a student). The departments slated for closure were among the most welcoming for Black faculty and students. To justify the departmental closings, the University President likened the administrator's decision to that of the Three-Fifths Compromise,[1] explaining that often compromises must be made for the greater good. These incidents and many more all occurred within a context of palpable pretentiousness in classes, at events, and on campus in general. And so I came undone.

Two decades after my children's chorus experience, my internal quest for justice remained intact. By adding dimensions of power, privilege, and oppression to my argument, the difference in how I was received by White people had changed dramatically. My perception of that change infuriated me, as I knew my principles had not changed. Alongside my anger, I felt a dark sadness and deep fear. Sadness because despite my lifelong experience of academic efficacy and earning high grades, I realized I had never developed the critical thinking skills necessary for graduate school. Though in retrospect I see it differently, at the time this realization made me question my schooling until that point. Had teachers just simply applauded my "abilities" because I was commonly the only Black student in high-level classes? Or worse, because I was "different" from most of the other Black students? Fear because I found myself in a "top-tier" university utterly underprepared. I stopped sleeping, for when I closed my eyes I began to see images of a gun blowing off the back portion of my brain. These images encroached on my daytime existence eventually; I began to see them when I blinked.

Determined to finish the program that I saw as my portal to spaces where I might affect educational change for Black and Brown kids, I doggedly trekked to the end. A year prior to completing the program and much to my surprise, I won what I had been trained to consider the ultimate prize: a tenure track job in a college of education. I was unfazed when some of my graduate school professors articulated their disappointment that I was not offered a position at a Research I school, as I deeply desired an exit from spaces seemingly defined by an ever-present push for more prestige and more power. My desire to leave one type of institution, however, did not mean I was prepared to enter a context with an entirely different brand of racism.

Crazy 999: Assistant Professorship

Only after I began as a junior faculty member at a regional comprehensive university did I realize that most of the interpersonal racism I had experienced until then had been guarded, cloaked in liberal politeness. Most often, the aforementioned systemic and interpersonal racism endemic to many elite universities took place alongside my being invited to fancy wine and cheese receptions. In my new context, I encountered White people who existed outside the boundaries of the elite university-associated White people among whom I had lived for much of my life. Unschooled in the subtleties of liberal White condescension – and often hostile to what they disparagingly termed "political correctness" – I had numerous interactions with colleagues and students that exacerbated my mental health diagnoses.

I was shocked when, for example, a White colleague barged into my class uninvited, interrupted me mid-sentence, and shouted to my (all White) students that I was "the cream of the crop" while hooking my neck in her elbow fold and pointing her other finger in my face. I was frustrated when a White colleague was promoted, despite my official reports that she frequently told racist "jokes" (e.g. warning us to get ready to eat frozen cat and dog if we met at a Korean American colleague's house). I was angry when Betty,[2] a White full professor serving on a search committee I was chairing, aggressively micro-managed me and insisted that I do things her way. I was incensed when she declared that a queer Black male applicant's work would "fit" in the nearby city, but certainly not in our suburban context.

At first, I thought I was effectively handling the microaggressions I faced almost daily. In truth, I was compartmentalizing the effects of the offenses in a manner that would eventually prove unmanageable. Because I lived in the city and commuted to the suburban university, I developed a process by which I would "armor up" on my 40-minute commute to work, and de-armor on my way home. Once home, I often shared stories of collegial interactions with my family and friends. Safely in the city, I was listened to and comforted; often my venting sessions ended in laughter as we reflected on my responses to the ridiculousness of my colleagues' assumptions.

During my third year, however, any illusion I previously had about the extent to which my compartmentalizing kept harm at bay was crushed. I tripped over the socially-defined boundary of sanity, which necessitated psychiatric hospitalization and a semester-long medical leave of absence. Prior to my medical leave, I had chosen not to address the offenders. The trauma of my time in the psych ward illuminated the cost of my silence. I came to understand that despite my desire to mitigate collegial microaggressions by simply "not giving them energy," I would have to address them directly. The alternative might kill me.

It took several semesters after my return to build back my strength, in part because the microaggressions did not cease. I had a lot to learn about confronting aggressors in a professional manner lest I showcase the magnitude of my anger. Though I had studied historical and contemporary oppression since middle school, my multiple privileges had rendered the topic theoretical until then.

In one particularly troubling episode, a member of the college leadership team shared her perception of the difference between a colleague named Crystal and me. She explained to me that while I was "kind, gentle," and "[took] it easy on White faculty" when they made racist comments, "Crystal [was]… bigger." In conjunction with her last word, she straightened her spine and formed her hands into fists in the manner that often accompanies describing someone who has visible brute strength.

At that moment, the myth of my mental wellness gave way (again). Had she really just compared me with my friend in that way? It matters to the story that I am 5'4", light skinned, wear my natural hair cut short and was still relatively soft-spoken at my institution. In comparison, Crystal is 5'11", chocolate, wears her natural hair longer, and asserted herself frequently in a firm and professional manner. I was equally incensed that my supervisor perceived me to be the "Good Negro" and that her observations of my friend drew on textbook stereotypes of the "Angry Black Woman." Although I was cognitively aware that it was not my responsibility to teach my colleagues why their interactions were so toxic, I found it hard not to respond as they revealed just how unaware they were.

Pedagogical Consequences

The influence these experiences had on my teaching that semester were direct and immense. My internal indignation flattened any remaining efficacy that I had regarding my ability to teach effectively. My White colleagues' ignorance bothered me most because they also taught pre- and inservice teachers. I was outraged that K-12 students would be learning from teachers who were taught by my racist colleagues. As a mode of self-preservation, I forced myself to go numb in my interactions with colleagues and students.

Attempting to heal my heart as the nation witnessed the mostly unpunished murders of Trayvon Martin, Mike Brown, John Crawford, Renisha McBride, Eric Garner, Ezell Ford, Tamir Rice, and Sandra Bland, among others was incredibly challenging. The first few times a student articulated the minutia of what "actually happened" when George Zimmerman killed Trayvon Martin, or the necessity for police officers to defend themselves, I realized I did not have the skills to facilitate nor model a productive conversation. My increased volume, narrowed eyes, and sharp condemnation affirmed the rage I felt. One effect of my craziness on my pedagogy, therefore, is that students are not given space to grapple with these difficult issues in class.

Searching for other avenues to reach my students led me to share my mental health challenges; lives lost due to silence weigh heavily on my soul. At the start of each semester, I introduce the concept of multiple identities to my students. Together, we brainstorm identity categories (race, gender, class, religion, physical ability, mental ability, etc.), using a graphic organizer with blank spaces for "Identity Categories," "My Identities," and "Groups with Systemic Power." Next, I ask my students to write down how they identify in each category. I then share my identities with them, writing "a little crazy" in the box that correlates with how I identify regarding mental ability. One of my aims in collectively filling out the third column, indicating which groups hold historical and contemporary power, is to showcase intersectionality and the complex interplay of power and oppression within most of us. Though a member of certain oppressed groups (as a Black/White biracial queer woman with mental illness), I am also a member of groups with systemic power (as a highly degreed, cisgender, able-bodied person from a family of origin with more than enough resources).

Regarding my battles with mental illness, many students have thanked me for my transparency: some confiding their own similar battles, others sharing stories of family members lost to suicide. I think these shared moments of vulnerability between my mostly White students and me has allowed for otherwise evasive levels of trust. My hope is that I can encourage these preservice teachers to investigate the messiness of their own multiple identities, including the areas they have been socialized to internalize shame. Perhaps this will help them be more vulnerable with their future K-12 students.

When Darren Wilson was not indicted for killing Mike Brown in November 2014, I flew to Missouri to join an NAACP-led march across the state called

"Journey for Justice." Our class had bonded closely that semester, due largely to my early mental health disclosure. Because the march took place during the last week of classes, I was able to be in close communication with my students throughout the experience. Upon my return, several students indicated that my participation in the march inspired them to get active. By sharing the meditative aspects of the march, I demystified the process by which I used footsteps' rhythms to ease my heart. One student, who early in the semester shyly confided in me that she also battles mental health issues, stayed after class on the final day. She tearfully expressed her appreciation for my demonstrating how to channel heartache into positive energy for social change.

Conclusion

Fanon's *Wretched of the Earth* helps me situate my "craziness" into the colonial reality within which it originated and festered. This, together with my lifelong critical consciousness, helps me teach through obstacles that once served as barriers to clear thought and mental wellness. By risking vulnerability, I reach for honesty: a place from which I can engage in transformative educational practices. By embracing the term "crazy" and confronting racism in K–12 schooling and in teacher education, I have developed tools for my own healing intersectionally. My students' exploration of their multiple identities may challenge their tendency to see their students as raced and classed while considering their own race, class (and other) identities as somehow neutral. A teacher's awareness of her own positionality – and how that positionality has shaped her perspectives – is a crucial component of understanding her future students and their families.

Notes

1 1787 U.S. federal legislation to settle disputes between northern and southern delegates regarding how to count enslaved Black people for congressional representation. The delegates agreed to count them at three-fifths of a person.
2 All proper nouns are pseudonyms.

References

Dimitriadis, G., Cole, E., & Costello, A. (2009). The social field(s) of arts education today: Living vulnerably in neo-liberal times. *Discourse: Studies in the Cultural Politics of Education 30*(4), 361–379.
Fanon, F. (1963). *Wretched of the Earth*. New York, NY: Grove Press.
Friere, P. (1970). *Pedagogy of the Oppressed*. New York, NY: Herder and Herder.
Laymon, K. (2013). *How to Slowly Kill Yourself and Others in America: Essays*. Chicago, IL: Bolden.
Lorde, A. (1984). *Sister Outsider*. New York, NY: Crown Publishing.
Macedo, D. (2000). Introduction. *Pedagogy of the Oppressed*. New York, NY: Bloomsbury Publishing.

9   Creating Equity Warriors in the Face of White Fragility

Alana D. Murray and Heather E. Yuhaniak

Desegregation brought us together. Heather Yuhaniak (White female instructional specialist) and I (Alana Murray, Black female administrator) met as teacher leaders hired to open a new suburban middle school funded by a federal desegregation grant to decrease socioeconomic isolation in a diverse, working class neighborhood. As one of the only people of Color on the team, I quickly became seen as the voice of dissent on our mostly White leadership team as we made myriad decisions involved in opening a new school. I tussled most frequently with an assistant principal who embodied the "White savior" (Vera & Gordan, 2003) mentality and regaled us with stories of how he connected effectively with Black male students. Though a product of and experienced educator in our district, my opinions about what would work best for our students of Color were quickly dismissed. My experience as a successful teacher of Color was erased and my intentions were constantly questioned.

Though neither of us had language for it at the time, what we faced on that team were regular demonstrations of what Robin DiAngelo (2011) deems "White fragility." The term encompasses a wide variety of behaviors and emotions displayed by Whites that are indicative of how "fragile and ill-equipped [they] are to confront racial tensions" (DiAngelo, 2011, p. 65). Sociologist Allen Johnson (2014) argues that discussions of race and White privilege are difficult even for the well-intentioned because they force us to acknowledge what's going on without inviting guilt and blame… the result is a knotted tangle of fear, anger, blame, defensiveness, guilt, pain, denial, ambivalence, and confusion" (p. 5). Rather than acknowledge the role that race plays in our ability to create educational policy and practice that would best serve our diverse school community, our White leaders pushed back on my attempts to question our replication of institutional racism in these decisions. As Lisa Delpit (1995) describes:

> When you're talking to White people they still want it to be their way. You can try to talk to them and give them examples, but they're so headstrong, they think they know what's best for everybody, for everybody's children.
>
> (p. 45)

This chapter examines how White fragility has impacted the arc of our careers and how we have leveraged ongoing interracial dialogue to work against White resistance and upset hegemonic norms in education.

Alana's Story

I began my work as a social justice educator at Brown University in the Master of Arts in Teaching program. I vividly recall my White classmates' frustrations about the lateness, the perceived lack of organization, and the lectures of an African American female professor. After many classes, they often huddled in order to commiserate about how the class did not provide them with tangible strategies to work with their students. Her students of Color, however, experienced the professor quite differently. We loved how she introduced all of her students to research generated by scholars of Color to frame questions about the experience of Black children in public schools.

I recall a White student sharing a story about how she understood the needs of a Black Latina girl based on one conversation she had with her after class. My professor challenged this student to address her savior stance by asking a simple question: "How do you know if this child is being honest with you?" The professor unsettled the White student's notion that she could understand the totality of the Black experience by one interaction with a student. Instead of praising the student for her response our professor attempted to push the student's thinking in a deeper direction. The student fumbled for a response and other White students attempted to answer for her. After class, the White students gathered to complain about why the professor asked a "mean" question that made this student feel uncomfortable. I was struck with how my White peers focused on their own emotions rather than grapple with a question designed to help them analyze how an African American child negotiated her own schooling experience. Their White emotion erased the professor's ability to provide content that would assist them in interacting effectively with their students of Color.

I too, like my professor, have felt "erased." In my roles as K-12 and teacher educator I've learned that navigating White fragility often renders Black educators either hypervisible or invisible. If I chose to speak up when my world history cohort centers the European experience in our curriculum, I invoke the trope of the "angry Black female" trying to "make everything about race." My colleagues react emotionally to my advocacy and I suspect they begin to see only my race in these conversations, not me. When structuring my syllabi for courses taught to mostly White preservice social studies teachers, I have to carefully select texts and learning experiences that will challenge them to not overlook the experiences of people of Color, rendering us invisible in the curriculum. While challenging institutional racism as an administrator in my current building, I feel compelled to build "buy in" by providing White staff the opportunity to discuss their fears and concerns prior to rolling out new initiatives related to closing the opportunity gap. If I do not carefully plan my entry into race conversations, they often become silent when talking about issues that face our Black and Latino students.

Choreographing my White colleague's emotional reactions to discussions of race takes an emotional toll on me. At points in my career, I sought mental health counseling to aid in traversing the negation of my experiences as a Black woman and how it left me emotionally spent. Here I learned strategies to use my emotional resources at work in healthy and productive ways. The undue burden placed on Black teachers and staff in school settings to confront White fragility possibly contributes to our declining presence in the profession in the post Brown v. Board of Education landscape.

Black educators face the unfair challenge of dismantling an educational system that oppresses us in order to create better conditions for minority children. My educational heroes Mary McLeod Bethune, Anna Julia Cooper, and Nannie H. Burroughs paved the way, fighting for Black children's education at the turn of the twentieth century. Like them, my need for deep and meaningful conversation about equitable outcomes for all students causes me to speak up and out. However, speaking up about racial justice issues is time consuming and unpopular. Often, I have felt compelled to silence my voice. And in those instances where I have not, I immediately became framed as "outspoken," "difficult to work with," and "angry." My struggles to deal with White fragility have had very real consequences for my career.

Heather's Story

I very well could have been one of the fragile White undergrads Alana described. I too would have struggled with a professor who did not adhere to my White preferences for promptness, action orientation, and quick-fix instructional strategies rather than critical conversation. Though both my high school and college experiences were steeped in Catholic notions of social justice, neither prepared me to struggle when faced with evidence negating my notions of our educational system as a colorblind meritocracy (Milner, 2012). My homogenous and racially privileged experiences left me impotent to meet the many and varied needs of the children of Color who greeted me in the classroom.

As a new teacher, I was the racial minority for the first time, and quickly invoked deficit narratives (Valencia, 2012) to explain my students' achievement data. Rather than grapple with my own deficient knowledge, skills, and dispositions needed to serve diverse students, I blamed what I at the time perceived to be their lack of skills, positive role models at home, and motivation. I lectured them about how hard work always equals success and consistently questioned their work ethic. I bought into false narratives about the "culture of poverty" (Payne, 2005) that led me to blame my own students for their poverty (Gorski, 2008). My anger and indignation transcended beyond my own classroom and found a target in Alana. As a fellow building leader, I feigned support throughout several professional development sessions about the impact of race on education (designed by her) and spent hours afterward "processing" (read: gossiping) with a White peer about what a complete waste of time we thought they were because of their narrow focus on race.

Luckily, the White savior administrator who Alana tussled with left, and our leadership team became more diverse. Our principal decided we would read Singleton and Linton's (2006) *Courageous Conversations about Race*. Our team divided up the chapters and took turns facilitating monthly discussions. Surprisingly, I looked forward to these sessions, and learned a great deal due to the evident planning that each person brought to his or her session, as well as the depth of commentary shared by my colleagues, especially those of Color.

As a White person new to racial dialogue, I frequently entered the conversation with a detached intellectual stance, seeking additional data and information about the topic at hand. My patient colleagues and friends, already burdened by their own oppression, added my naiveté to their load and helped me shift my reactions to race. They willingly shared counterstories (Solórzano & Yosso, 2001) about their own backgrounds and educational experiences with me and I began to unpack my colorblind and deficit ideologies, recognizing my own fragility when confronted with race. I began to examine ways in which my classroom management reinforced White dominant norms (Katz, 1978) and preferenced individualism, quiet, and order, instead of culturally reflective pedagogy including collective learning and cooperation, and authentic dialogue instead of silent compliance. I rethought the many times I had scolded Black girls to be quieter in the halls, but remained completely oblivious to rowdy groups of White teens. I felt shame at pushing students out of my classroom and depriving them of instruction due to their misbehavior while parroting a belief that ALL students can succeed.

I must constantly seek to re-center myself in my work as a teacher educator. My emotions no longer stem from fragility about discussing race and its impact, but instead are triggered by my White colleague's own expressions of the very ideologies I once engaged. I strive for patience and humility with both them, and myself, for I know that an autonomous White racial identity is indeed a journey, not a destination, and if I was able to get there at times, then my White colleagues and program participants can as well. *It a choice that requires courage.*

Our Story: Confronting Fragility in Teacher Education

Though discussions of race often evoke complex feelings in people of all backgrounds, these emotional reactions often embody fragility for Whites. The widening demographic divide between a predominantly White teaching force and an increasingly non-White student population presents an exigent imperative for teacher educators to facilitate meaningful dialogue around race and its import in education. As colleagues and teacher educators,

Heather and I (Alana) were not always able to have productive interracial dialogue about the very real manifestations of institutional racism plaguing our suburban school. Her White fragility stymied our work. For example, our principal assigned us to collaboratively plan and lead professional learning for the social studies department, which I chaired. As a former social studies teacher herself, Heather initially failed to see why I constantly pushed new initiatives like National History Day and the Black Saga Club on my already (in her opinion) overburdened teachers. She could not wrap her head around how our "pobrecitos," who had escaped war, gang involvement, and more in their home countries could possibly rise to the level of rigor demanded by such intellectual challenges. Her false pride about opting to work in schools with majority students of Color masked the unexamined and unrelenting pity she felt for our students, which led her to consequently lower her academic and life expectations for them. She did not share this with me at the time, and appeared supportive of my attempts to move more students of Color into advanced classes, even in the middle of the semester. She masked her fragility with White silence, leaving me to lead our group in providing children of Color with opportunities to access rigorous intellectual curricula that enabled them to grow academically.

I made a cautious and careful choice in enlisting Heather's help in the design of a graduate certificate in equity and excellence in education. Though she had previously dismissed my voice on our leadership team, I knew she had skills in creating professional development and a strong work ethic. In my career, I have learned not to trust the intentions of all the White people with whom I work. In the most recent era of educational reform many White educators have made careers out of analyzing communities of Color from a deficit perspective. My career has been replete with White teachers who "saw themselves as kindhearted people who were doing right by the less fortunate and students who struggled to maintain their culture and identity while being forced to be the type of student their teacher envisioned" (Emdin, 2016, p. 4). As a Black educator I reject these savior types. I look to collaborate with White educators who understand their own White identity journey, who exhibit an ability to trust my story, who accept that my experience with children of Color is valid and who demonstrate an unyielding commitment to end racism in the United States. The more that we collaborated closely in designing instruction for our middle school and adult students, the more I saw Heather begin to exhibit these qualities.

As a White person struggling with my own racial identity, this interracial collaboration gave me (Heather) license to talk openly about race, and more importantly, to listen and learn from Alana's experiences. Not surprisingly, our ongoing dialogue triggered cognitive dissonance in me as a White person, which presented itself in my desire to withdraw, through silence, from the conversations. Interracial dialogue often results in the prioritization of White learning at the expense and re-victimization of people of Color who share their experiences with race and racism (Sensoy & DiAngelo,

2014). Alana had clearly advanced to a place in her own racial identity development where she could handle my questions and comments, and even sometimes silence, with grace. *force!* -

Her faith in me as a co-designer, instructor, and eventual coordinator of the certificate program was appreciated but completely undeserved. Our intention was to enable inservice educators to provide multilayered and critical approaches to teaching. We developed courses that start with an examination of personal identities, shift to classroom practices, and culminate with participants addressing inequities in their school buildings and beyond. In leading others in this challenging work, I felt like a complete farce. I had only recently begun to process my own racial identity and ideologies and struggled to stay ahead of the students with course readings. I contributed structures and processes to our lesson plans, but felt devoid of the content knowledge and passion that Alana brought to our shared work. I remained woefully uneducated about the core topics of race, privilege, oppression, and social justice to which students are exposed in the program. Unexpectedly, I ended up co-teaching the rest of the courses in the sequence with her and continue to do so to this day.

Conclusion

Our shared mission as teacher educators is to facilitate participants' development of the knowledge, skills, and dispositions necessary to change the landscape for our students in a rapidly re-segregating school district. Our collaboration is what enabled Heather to develop these herself. At the heart of our shared story is constant, ongoing interracial dialogue. Though it was not always this way, we barely make it through a day without a text, email, or late night phone call once kids, spouses, and pets are tucked away for the night. Our now-friendship functions as what Leonardo (2009) calls the "third space," in which Whites operate as "neither enemy or ally but a concrete subject of struggle" (p. 186). This co-constructed third space remains "guided by [Alana's] non-White discourses" (Leonardo, 2009, p. 186) and supports Heather's development of a "nuanced understanding of [her] racialized self" (Utt & Tochluk, 2016, p. 4). Successfully navigating Heather's colorblindness and fragility together has afforded us a unique perspective on how to foster our White participants' racial identity development, including how best to help them "understand their own and other individuals' racial background, racial heritage, and consequences of race that cause oppression and privilege" (Milner, 2003, p. 207). We sustain ourselves as partners through this work in the same way that we tackle fragility with our adult students and colleagues: through open, honest, interracial dialogue that always aims to unpack the inequities that surround us and our struggle to disrupt them.

Love Happy Ending

80   *Alana D. Murray and Heather E. Yuhaniak*

References

Delpit, L. (1995). *Other People's Children: Cultural conflict in the classroom.* New York, NY: The New Press.

DiAngelo, R. (2011). White fragility. *International Journal of Critical Pedagogy, 3*(3), 54–70.

Emdin, C. (2016). *For White Folks Who Teach in the Hood... and the Rest of Y'all Too: Reality pedagogy and urban education.* Boston, MA: Beacon Press.

Gorski, P. (2008). The myth of the 'culture' of poverty. *Educational Leadership, 65*(7), 32.

Johnson, A. G. (2014). *The Gender Knot: Unraveling our patriarchal legacy.* Philadelphia, PA: Temple University Press.

Katz, J. H. (1978). *White Awareness: Handbook for antiracism training.* Norman, OK: University of Oklahoma Press.

Leonardo, Z. (2009). *Race, Whiteness, and Education.* New York, NY: Routledge.

Milner IV, H. R. (2003). Reflection, racial competence, and critical pedagogy: How do we prepare pre-service teachers to pose tough questions? *Race Ethnicity and Education, 6,* 193–208.

Milner IV, H. R. (2012). Beyond a test score: Explaining opportunity gaps in educational practice. *Journal of Black Studies, 43*(6), 693–718. doi: 10.1177/0021934712442539

Payne, R. K. (2005). *A Framework for Understanding Poverty.* Highlands, TX: Aha! Process.

Sensoy, Ö., & DiAngelo, R. (2014). Respect differences? Challenging the common guidelines in social justice education. *Democracy and Education, 22*(2), 1.

Singleton, G. E., & Linton, C. (2006). *Courageous Conversations about Race: A field guide for achieving equity in schools.* Thousand Oaks, CA: Corwin Press.

Solórzano, D. G., & Yosso, T. J. (2001). From racial stereotyping and deficit discourse toward a critical race theory in teacher education. *Multicultural Education, 9*(1), 2–8.

Utt, J., & Tochluk, S. (2016). White teacher, know thyself: Improving anti-racist praxis through racial identity development. *Urban Education,* 1–28. doi: 0042085916648741

Valencia, R. R. (Ed.). (2012). *The Evolution of Deficit Thinking: Educational thought and practice.* New York, NY: Routledge.

Vera, H., & Gordan, A. (2003). *Screen Saviors: Hollywood fictions of whiteness.* Lanham, MD: Rowman and Littlefield.

10 You Just Don't See Me!

The "Puerto Rico Incident" and the Choice of Freedom from Silence

Noemí Cortés

In the office foyer, myself and a White male colleague, Jim,[1] engaged in a heated dispute. After vetting many candidates, my supervisor, a woman of *Un* Color, was prepared to offer the position for my new co-teacher to the *only* *believable* candidate who met *all* of the qualifications for the position: the Black male candidate. She and I agreed that his experience and our compatibility as co-instructors made him the top candidate. Jim adamantly disagreed and insisted I support his stance: this candidate needed to return for further questioning. I would not relent in my opposition. As all of our colleagues watched, including our program director, we argued. Eventually, someone interjected and we were all sent off to our students' end of year celebration.

At the celebration I realized I needed to pump my breast milk. I was a new mother, still nursing a four-month-old infant; therefore, I found the darkest, most isolated corner of our room, covered myself, and began pumping. At that moment Jim approached. He stood over me, pointing his finger in my face, and threatened to ensure the offer would never be made if I did not comply with his request to "re-interview" the Black male candidate. I repeated several times that he needed to leave, but he persisted; and I could not move. Again, students and colleagues watched; no one intervened. After years of racial aggression, I could not contain my rage. In the most belligerent way I could muster, I told him to leave. He looked at me and said, "Okay… it's your choice."

Overwhelmed by doubt, I wondered: is it possible to work as a racial justice educator of Color in a White-dominated institution of higher learning?

"Who" or "What" Are You?

On more than one occasion, I have been asked, "Where are you from?" My curly hair, brown skin, and Spanish accent when I say my name seems to leave the inquisitor unsatisfied with the response that I am from a major, urban U.S. city. The follow-up question is almost always, "What are you?" And while the obvious response is that "what I am" is human, the answer sought is distinctly tied to my heritage. I have been asked this question hundreds of times but have only recently come to understand that for many people of Color, the struggle for our humanity begins with this question; this need to label us as "other." The question does not begin with personhood (i.e. "Who" are you), but with our dehumanization (i.e. "What" are you). If I cannot simply be human, I need to give some other answer to justify the inquirer's racialized treatment of me.

So *who* am I? I am a Puerto Rican woman that attended public schools but was educated by a community of radical Boricuas. Where I am from is a place where systemic racism and oppression exists; a place where housing and economic segregation is so pervasive it continues to fuel racial tension between communities. For sixteen years I have oriented my teaching with a belief in racial justice for myself and my students. Nine years ago my work extended into the university setting.

The University Climate

I was employed by an institution that declared "social justice activism" – activism against structural inequities – as one of its core values. As staff we prioritized this ideal in coursework, teaching lessons on the manifestations of privilege, oppression, and racism in society and in our classrooms. Despite our program's purported social justice orientation, my White colleagues were dismissive of the pervasiveness of racial microaggressions – subtle, sometimes unconscious, verbal, or non-verbal insults directed at people of Color (Smith, Yossa, & Solórzano, 2006) – in our program. As the only Latina on staff, I was often positioned as having expertise in the field of language learning and supporting Latino students, but dismissed the moment the conversation turned to any other topic, including the pragmatics of teaching. It was not uncommon for my White colleagues to sit in my office and ask my opinion on how to support a Latino student "struggling with the language demands of the course" then turn to a White colleague to ask for resources regarding classroom management. My students (i.e. teacher candidates) often did the same; I was a resource in learning how to approach a Latina mother but my White colleague was their resource for learning how to teach math. My White colleagues rejected my claims that these actions were examples of microaggressions and proposed "logical" explanations as an alternative (Sue et al., 2007).

I was not alone in this experience. Many of our students of Color shared stories about the microaggressions they experienced during class; the ways they were devalued and objectified. Students reported White instructors making statements such as, "behind every good household is a good maid" and spotlighting students of Color to discuss what it is like to grow up poor, the child of immigrant parents, or some other deficit-laden stereotype. Just as I was positioned as expert in all things Latino, so too were my students of Color positioned as experts on racism and classism and dismissed as unknowledgeable in other areas.

These forms of racism are disorienting, particularly in a space that identifies itself as justice oriented with peers who purport to hold similar beliefs about racial justice. In reality, we were surrounded by "deceived perpetrators/ activist" (Young, 2011, p. 1447): White people so blinded by their definition of social justice, antiracist education that they are unwilling to see how *they* were actively committing racist acts. These were not overt acts of racism, but microaggressions; and as such it became difficult to confidently say that what was experienced was racist. In the moment, the statement or the look triggers you; sometimes you respond but more often you stay silent, stewing with the nagging feeling that your humanity has been devalued (Sue et al., 2007).

The Puerto Rico Incident

In our teacher preparation program, the moment when people of Color broke their silence came during a time our staff called "the Puerto Rico incident." The incident began when a White male student took a board game called *Puerto Rico* to an end of trimester celebration for the children of Color he was teaching. *Puerto Rico* is a game where players "assume the roles of colonial governors… and amass points by constructing buildings" such as plantations that must be manned by colonists (Puerto Rico, n.d., p. 1). This seemingly innocuous decision – identifying a board game with colonization as the theme as "fun" for children of Color – in fact, trivialized the horrific experiences of indigenous genocide, slavery, and colonization in Puerto Rico.

Students of Color, whose cumulative trauma with racism in this program was triggered by this incident, wanted to discuss their peer's decision. But their calls for dialogue were rejected by White instructors who declared the incident a "simple mistake." Instructors insisted everyone move forward; pushing for dialogue was making the offending (White) student feel "unsafe" and emotionally distraught (Leonardo & Porter, 2010). As their pleas for dialogue went ignored, students of Color began to feel as though their safety and trauma was irrelevant to program officials.

Students and staff of Color used the incident and the response of White staff to highlight the institution's culture of racism and White supremacy by naming to university directors White protectionism, institutional racism, and racial microaggressions within the program. These claims were met with resistance and resulted in intense tension between and among staff and students. The institution prided itself on valuing progressive liberal beliefs about racial justice. My White colleagues perceived themselves as "allies," as White people participating actively in the struggle against oppression. Yet, in this incident staff debated whose needs warranted a response by the program. The institution determined that the healing staff and students of Color needed from the psychological suffering they experienced as a result of constant racial hostility – our racial battle fatigue (Smith et al., 2006) – was not the central issue. Instead, university leaders instructed staff to protect the White student from his peers' frustrations by returning to "normal;" to teach course content without referencing "the incident" or other potentially contentious topics. This response, unconscious or not, was the perpetuation of racism by our institution (Young, 2011).

My Humanity or My Silence?

A supervisor offered me an opportunity to take a step toward healing from my own trauma by speaking solely to White staff and students and sharing how I was experiencing the Puerto Rico incident. I was immediately overwhelmed. I wondered whether objectifying myself for White people's learning was worth the emotional toll of telling my story. Experience told me this would be an academic lesson; another theoretical discussion on microaggressions and racism. As the only Puerto Rican in the program, I knew I was being spotlighted; but I couldn't shake the nagging feeling that this was the time to break my silence.

I reflected deeply on the expectations I had of my students; the constant reminders to them that the struggle for racial justice in education is an emotional journey that requires vulnerability and authenticity with children. However, in the back of my mind sat the fear and hesitation that overwhelms the heart when it becomes time to confront racism. But, I saw the opportunity of vulnerability and self-disclosure in a classroom (Kishimoto & Mwangi, 2009); a "teachable moment." Despite my fear, in a room full of my White colleagues and our White students I chose to assert my humanity. Tearfully, I explained why a board game that turned centuries of colonization and enslavement of my people into entertainment and "fun" is hurtful and harmful. I shared why our response as instructors needed to be about helping our students see this incident and its aftermath as a human experience and not solely an academic lesson (Matias, 2013). I expressed frustration in our program's inability to enact our values, but maintained that the opportunity to act was not lost.

Immediately afterward, division among staff intensified. White staff became angry and hostile. In meetings and private conversations, they declared that centering the needs of students and staff of Color in any dialogue above the needs of maintaining harmony across the program was selfish and divisive. A few weeks later first and second year elementary and secondary students organized a protest to declare their stance toward the institution. They marched into class and collectively stood in front of the entire staff. Students of Color gave testimony to acts of racism and the trauma they experienced in the program. White students who stood in solidarity decried the hypocrisy of the institution. Together, students resisted calls for their own compliance, threatening to publicly expose the program's racism if their demands for changes and the general de-centering of whiteness were not met.

Shortly thereafter, Jim aggressively stood over me at the celebration insisting upon my compliance.

My Humanity or My Compliance?

As people of Color, we are often forced to choose between our silence and our humanity. There are repercussions for both: the choke-hold of silence that leads us to remain paralyzed in the face of injustice or the retribution of the institution for having the audacity to reclaim our humanity (Leonardo & Porter, 2010). I made the choice to reclaim my humanity by standing with my students and calling for the institution to live up to its creed, but our words made those in power angry and the institution retaliated with impunity.

The institution determined that staff did not need to address the trauma of students and staff of Color. Staff was expected to protect White students and White staff from the emotional response their actions caused. I was reminded that my role as an employee of this institution was to "get on board" with this decision regardless of my stance; my compliance and my silence became the conditions for my continued employment. This expectation was reinforced when my "overseer" director (Córdova, 1998), a woman of Color espousing racial justice rhetoric without the will or courage to speak out against racism, apologized to all the White staff on behalf of all the staff of Color; and all the self-proclaimed White antiracist educators tacitly accepted her apology. Despite valuing "social justice activism," White staff rejected my calls for dialogue. Instead they cried, declaring they were afraid to speak to me.

For aligning with students instead of program authorities I was called into several closed-door meetings with various directors about the role of true leaders: their ability to move forward without being emotional. I was accused of "poor judgment" for trying to open dialogue; the possibility of my influencing more discord through dialogue was a threat to the perceived harmony that existed prior to the Puerto Rico incident (Córdova, 1998). Although I formally documented my anxiety and discomfort with Jim, my emotional distress was disregarded when my supervisor instructed me to forgive him for his aggressive behavior at the celebration. Just as he had threatened, the Black male candidate was not hired. Jim was assigned as my temporary co-teacher and continued as my officemate.

My Humanity!

My process of healing began with the realization that I needed to engage a humanizing pedagogy, one that prioritizes the development of caring and trusting relationships alongside sociopolitical consciousness (Bartolome, 1994). Since my program would not offer a restorative space for healing, I needed to create it. Despite the institution's opposition, I invited students to speak with me privately to express their concerns. We explicitly discussed the climate in our program prior to and after the Puerto Rico incident. These conversations, alongside other dialogues, were critical. By having the courage to remain in dialogue I learned from many students of Color that they felt marginalization and isolation so deeply they considered leaving the program. These conversations also revealed that my White students were unsure of my capacity to be objective in my evaluation of them; one specifically talked about feeling "unsafe" in my presence. She perceived that I had been "violent" in my words.

It is my belief that by dedicating myself to my pedagogy, my students and I developed a deeper sense of what it means to be a racial justice educator. We learned to be open with each other about our struggles in identifying and interrupting the racism we witnessed or experienced. Students of Color discovered ways to assert their voice, evidenced by their own choice to confront instructors and administrators about microaggressions. Although not all students were open to continued dialogue with each other or with staff, many chose to push their peers and instructors; challenging, in particular, simplistic notions of love in classrooms with children of Color and reemphasizing the importance of critically analyzing their own positionality.

Freedom from Silence

Jim believes himself to be an antiracist educator, but his action in the dark *disgist* corner of that room was not a display of ally-ship. It was an act of aggression; a response to the audacity of a Puerto Rican woman declaring that the self-proclaimed antiracist White educators and the "social justice" institution were agents of racism. Jim sought to demand my conformity and the institution required my compliance for continued employment. To stand in opposition to these demands was an affront to Jim's sense of self and the institution's identity.

But Jim is simply an archetype; one example of the hypocrisy of White antiracism in institutions. Many students and I found ways to enact a more racial justice oriented vision of our work, but our pushes did not radically change the hypocrisy in our institution. It remained a place where silence and compliance were rewarded and resistance resulted in marginalization and punishment. However, I no longer doubt whether I can work as a racial justice educator in a White-dominated institution of higher learning; it is inevitable that my work must occupy these spaces. Instead, this experience served as a reminder that working in these institutions will often require people of Color to make a choice: our humanity or our silence and compliance. While compliance may lead to employment security, it will not free us from our fear of retribution from our administrators or colleagues or result in racial justice.

I leave this experience resolute in saying: let us (people of Color) stand collectively to expose the racism we see and experience in our institutions. Let us build spaces where we can heal with each other, learn together, and regain the strength we need to reenter spaces that are hostile toward us and our pedagogy. We cannot sit, patiently waiting for an institution to prioritize our needs above its own. We must assert our humanity, despite the paralyzing fear of retribution, because "who" we are matters more than "what" we represent to the institution.

Note

1   The name is a pseudonym used for anonymity.

References

Bartolome, L. (1994). Beyond the methods fetish: Toward a humanizing pedagogy. *Harvard Educational Review, 64*(2), 173–194.

Córdova, T. (1998). Power and knowledge: Colonialism in the academy. *Living Chicana Theory.* Berkeley, CA: Third Woman Press.

Kishimoto, K., & Mwangi, M. (2009). Critiquing the rhetoric of "safety" in feminist pedagogy: Women of Color offering an account of ourselves. *Feminist Teacher, 19*(2), 87–102.

Leonardo, Z., & Porter, R. (2010). Pedagogy of fear: Toward a Fanonian theory of 'safety' in race dialogue. *Race Ethnicity and Education, 13*(2), 139–157.

Matias, C. (2013). On the "flip" side: A teacher educator of Color unveiling the dangerous minds of White teacher candidates. *Teacher Education Quarterly, 40*(2), 53–73.

Puerto Rico. (n.d.). In *Boardgamegeek.* Retrieved June 7, 2016, from https://boardgamegeek.com/boardgame/3076/puerto-rico

Smith, W., Yossa, T., & Solórzano, D. (2006). Challenging racial battle fatigue on historically White campuses: A critical race examination of race-related stress. In C. A. Stanley (Ed.), *Faculty of Color: Teaching in predominately White colleges and universities* (pp. 299–327). Bolton, MA: Anker Publishing.

Sue, D. W., Capodilupo, C., Torino, G., Bucceri, J., Holder, A., Nadal, K. L., & Esquilin, M. (2007). Racial microaggressions in everyday life: Implications for clinical practice. *American Psychologist, 62*(4), 271–286.

Young, E. (2011). The four personae of racism: Educators' (mis)understanding of individual versus systemic racism. *Urban Education,* 46(6), 1433–1460.

Part III
Building for Transformation

Lust favorite puppet loved it

11 Black Teacher Educator, White Teacher Interns

How I Learned to Bring My Whole Self to My Work

Tanya Maloney

"If a huge bear was coming at me, I would try to protect myself too!" Jeremy's emphatic words knocked me temporarily unconscious and an angry heat filled my body as I listened to my student, a future urban teacher, compare a Black adolescent to an animal. Jeremy, a White American male in his early twenties, had just completed the summer semester of a one-year urban teacher preparation program. For the first fall meeting of our fieldwork seminar, I asked him and his fellow interns, mostly White and Latina, to draft a script for how they would respond if one of their students asked them, "So, what do you think about this Michael Brown issue?" Michael Brown, a heavy-set Black teenager, had died that summer at the hands of a White police officer in Ferguson, a low income community just outside St. Louis, Missouri. The #BlackLivesMatter movement – a call to action after the disconcerting acquittal of Trayvon Martin's killer – gained momentum when Michael's death sparked nationwide demonstrations protesting police brutality in Black communities. Jeremy's script focused on Michael's size and his reported aggressive behavior, as Jeremy claimed not to see race as a major motivating factor in the officer's actions. In class, Jeremy explained that he thought the police officer might have been justified if Michael Brown had indeed threatened the officer's life. Jeremy also shared his thoughts on the demonstrations, "No one really knows exactly what happened, so I don't know why people are protesting. That doesn't seem productive."

This conversation represented one of many moments in which I realized I was centering race and racism in a way that my interns were not. As a Black woman born and raised in America, I could only see the officer's actions as inhumane and racially motivated. I am a second generation college graduate and the beneficiary of parents who achieved the "American dream" by attending college and buying a house. Perhaps the greatest privilege my parents bestowed upon me was raising me in a quiet, suburban neighborhood with excellent public schooling and positive relations between law enforcement and the few Black families in the community. Though I had these positive experiences in my own life, I shared a collective identity, peoplehood, or "fictive kinship" with all Black Americans, regardless of their socioeconomic status or social context (Fordham, 1996, p. 72). I grew up listening to my parents and family members express elation, shame, and disappointment for Black people they never met. I grew up believing that my accomplishments and failures would affect a larger community of Black people. Michael Brown's murder triggered a similar sadness, frustration, and fear within me as it did for the Ferguson community members. I understood why they rioted.

When Jeremy shared his perspective on the events surrounding Michael Brown's death, my world slowed down and multiple, conflicting thoughts rushed into my head. My intellectual being sought to patiently help Jeremy analyze his conceptions of institutional racism and to enlighten him on our country's preservation of state violence on Black bodies. I believed that as a young White man, Jeremy must have lived so positively affected by racism, classism, and patriarchy that he was oblivious to the experiences of poor people of Color. While my scholarly mind kept me calm, my blackness wanted to jump out of my seat and use loud, unprofessional words to reveal the emotions Jeremy stirred up within me. I was concerned for how Jeremy would approach his larger Black male students. Would they all be "bears" waiting to be provoked? Could they have a fair chance in his classroom as students? I also wondered if he would trust me, his Black teacher educator, to help him explore these questions.

In my moment of contemplation, I noticed the interns waiting for me to respond to Jeremy's statements. He had just expressed multiple microaggressions about poor, Black male adolescents, so I tried to create space for the other interns to share how they were feeling about his brief, and likely unintentional insults (Sue et al., 2007). "How do others feel about what Jeremy is saying?" I asked. I still felt the aftershock of his remarks and was unsure of how my emotions might spill into the dialogue, so I avoided participating in the conversation and turned to the class for their thoughts. I hoped Anthony would come to my rescue as he had throughout the summer semester.

Anthony, a White American male, previously shared his experiences growing up in a community he perceived to be conscious of racism and other forms of oppression. He revealed that he took the online *Harvard Implicit Association Test*[1] and that his results revealed that even *he* had unexamined biases, despite his otherwise socially aware family and neighborhood. In one class meeting during the previous semester, we discussed the concept of White privilege, or the set of advantages from which White people benefit on a daily basis. Jeremy expressed that because he was not rich, he did not understand how he could be considered *privileged*. Anthony interjected, "I think what Tanya is saying is that because we're White men, there are a lot of ways in which people treat us differently than people of Color." I saw Anthony's response caused Jeremy to pause and consider how his white skin might afford him privileges of which he was not previously aware. Anthony continued to affirm my statements all summer. He was clear about how we all harbor implicit bias and how these ideas could affect our teaching practice.

Anthony became my White ally in the classroom, someone I could turn to when I needed someone to reinforce my statements and repeat them with a White voice, in this case, a White male voice.

I called on Anthony. "Why don't they wait to see what the courts say before they jump to any conclusions and riot? They're just ruining their own neighborhood." As Anthony supported Jeremy, I lost the White ally I had had just a few months prior. Abandoned and viscerally experiencing the microaggressions from my students, the angry heat continued to well within me. It perplexed me that Anthony could have voiced an understanding of White privilege, institutional racism, and bias, but not recognize the range in ways racism could engender rioting within a community of frustrated Black citizens where racial profiling recently led to the murder of an unarmed Black teenager. I remained silent, hoping another intern would push back on either Jeremy or Anthony. Then, Naomi, a Latina intern in her early twenties, raised her hand. I called on her hoping she would disrupt the "overwhelming presence of Whiteness" that had taken over the room (Sleeter, 2001, p. 101). She shared her thoughts on how police officers should patrol areas that are considered more dangerous than other neighborhoods. I sat stunned as I listened to one of my few students of Color reinforce whiteness. A groupthink defined by dominant racial ideologies had revealed itself in our classroom and I realized that I might be the only dissenting voice. I took a deep breath and tried to respond with intellect instead of emotion.

I told Jeremy and Anthony they were operating from the assumption that the judicial system is fair and just for all Americans and asked them to think if they really believed that was the case. I suggested to Naomi, "If the police patrol certain areas excessively, then the crime rate is bound to increase in those areas, thus making them appear to be 'dangerous.'" I shared Michelle Fine's participatory action research on the disproportionate numbers of stop-and-frisk cases in Black neighborhoods in Manhattan as compared to wealthier, White areas in the same city (Stoudt, Fine, & Fox, 2011). In sharing her work, I made Fine my new White ally, and I was no longer confronting the interns' dominant ideologies on my own. Foregrounding others' scholarship also allowed me to avoid sharing my personal thoughts about the interns' ideas. This move required less of my own emotional investment and allowed me to practice self-care at a time when I was still feeling wearied by the microaggressions I was experiencing in my own classroom.

Attempting to Disrupt Hegemonic Understandings

The initial script-writing exercise and subsequent class discussion revealed the interns' hegemonic understandings and colorblind ideologies. They justified and supported the over-policing of Black communities and even Michael Brown's death. The interns' colorblind discourse took on frames of "minimization of race" and "cultural racism" (Bonilla-Silva, 2006, p. 26). Their ideas stemmed from their hegemonic understandings of "fear" and

"Whites as victims" (Picower, 2009, p. 202). In her study looking at White, female, preservice teachers in their twenties, Picower (2009) found her participants were often operating from a place of fearing people of Color, particularly African Americans, and that White people often see *themselves* as the victims of racism.

The interns' conceptions of racism disheartened me, but I remained optimistic of their growth because the fieldwork seminar included various readings and assignments that were intended to push their thinking about race, class, and urban communities. We read a chapter from Massey and Denton's (1993) *American Apartheid: Segregation and the Making of the Underclass* to discuss the ways in which racially segregated housing practices led to the creation and persistence of poverty for Black people in America. We read Jean Anyon's (1980) piece, "Social Class and the Hidden Curriculum of Work" and discussed terms such as "cultural capital" and "social reproduction." Gloria Ladson-Billings, Dianne Ravitch, Lisa Delpit, and Howard Stevenson each appeared on the syllabus. The interns completed weekly reflections, called critical incidents, in which they wrote about an event that surprised them or prompted them to reevaluate their own thinking about an issue. Racism, classism, heteronormativity, and other forms of oppression remained at the center of all of the readings and class activities.

Throughout the semester, Jeremy's critical incidents were often about classroom decisions such as why his collaborating teacher decided to discipline a particular student or how poorly his students performed on an assignment. He asked important questions about discipline, curriculum, and testing, but I hoped he would eventually identify the ways in which race or class might influence his experiences. I hesitated to ask him to consider the racial implications throughout his reflections. I recalled my previous experiences with White teacher candidates and their expressed exhaustion with ongoing conversations about race. Instead of addressing Jeremy directly, I looked across the critical incidents each week and raised broad questions to the whole group. I continued to practice self-care by letting the interns in the room share their thoughts instead of exposing my own. I did not confront Jeremy in any direct manner in order to avoid creating any tension between us. I also did not want to ask him a question that would lead to a response that could potentially cause me to experience the same discomfort I felt on the first day of class.

Instead of probing him, I thought the final assignment for the semester would encourage Jeremy to confront some of his conceptions about race, as it required the interns to complete a comprehensive community study. The study included statistics about racial demographics and average income as well as local school performance data. The interns also needed to learn about their students by participating in activities such as a school-based student club meeting, volunteering in the community, or riding the local bus line. The information they gathered would inform a culturally relevant lesson they would plan and enact in their classroom.

Jeremy completed the statistical analysis with detail and chose to interact with a few of his students in his classroom in order to fulfill the latter part of the assignment. I was disappointed that Jeremy did not venture outside of the comfort of his school to learn more about his students' community as a way to inform his instruction. In my feedback to him I wrote, "While I appreciate hearing about your conversation with your students, for this project I wanted you to be more intentional about how you were going beyond the school walls to learn something new about your students." He did not respond to this comment, but he was not required to do so. My direct feedback was likely too little and too late as Jeremy was not obligated to return to the project and engage differently. I do not think he reflected on his conceptions of race and racism in ways that I hoped he would. However, I remained encouraged after reading his concluding reflection, within which he expressed regret for not guiding his students toward taking on any social activism. Though Jeremy's initial ideas about racism and social justice became more complex, he seemed to avoid any explicit discussion about racial inequity in his lessons with his students. I ended the semester wondering how I needed to develop as a teacher educator in order to deepen my students' antiracist teaching practices, while also acknowledging the greater hegemonic forces that worked against all of us.

Bringing My Whole Self

The ever-present nature of racism means hegemonic ideology not only influences K-12 teaching and learning, but my university classroom as well. Talking about race and racism with a group of White and Latina preservice teachers often felt like an awkward dance. At the same time that my students feared they would say something that would uncover their racist thinking, I avoided stating my own ideas as I was unsure of where my students would draw the line between effective teacher educator and angry Black woman. I wanted all of my students to feel comfortable sharing their honest thoughts about race as well as class, gender, sexuality, and ability. In order to maintain a sense of comfort for my students, I kept my own thoughts to myself. I tried to ignore the emotional pain of being a Black woman listening to White men compare Black boys to animals. By not sharing, I assumed I approached the interns as a *raceless*, and perhaps even *genderless*, teacher educator. To think I could possibly come to class without my race and gender was enacting the very colorblind practice I did not want to see the interns portray in their classrooms. To express my Black womanhood would offer the interns an experience considered rare in the overwhelmingly White field of teacher preparation. I would also not want my silence to inadvertently affirm some of the hegemonic messages voiced in our classroom.

As I move forward, I will need to build empathy and affirm trust with future interns by first trusting them with my story. This will require me to unapologetically forefront my consistent focus on race and racism at the start of each semester. I must explain how the coursework intends to develop interns' multifaceted racial identity (Maloney, 2015) and, as such, will interrogate not only institutional racism, but also internalized and personally mediated, or relational racism (Jones, 2000). I would also situate myself as a learner and thus a participant in the discussions and share my own views on discussions. If I expect the interns to learn to teach toward liberation, then I must find the fine line between calling out their colorblind discourse and building their trust in me as their Black teacher educator by bringing my whole self to this work.

Note

1 The Implicit Association Test (IAT) measures attitudes and beliefs that people may be unwilling or unable to report. The IAT measures the strength of associations between concepts (e.g. Black people, gay people) and evaluations (e.g. good, bad) or stereotypes (e.g. athletic, clumsy). The test is online here: https://implicit.harvard.edu/implicit/education.html

References

Anyon, J. (1980). Social class and the hidden curriculum of work. *Journal of Education*, *52*(1), 67–93.

Bonilla-Silva, E. (2006). *Racism without Racists: Color-blind racism and the persistence of racial inequality in the United States*. Lanham, MD: Rowman & Littlefield Publishers.

Fordham, S. (1996). *Blacked Out: Dilemmas of race, identity, and success at Capital High*. Chicago, IL: University of Chicago Press.

Jones, C. P. (2000). Levels of racism: A theoretic framework and a gardener's tale. *American Journal of Public Health*, *90*(8), 1212–1215.

Maloney, T. (2015). The impact of the Teach For America experience on emerging leaders (Doctoral dissertation). Retrieved from *ProQuest*. Paper AAI3704041. http://repository.upenn.edu/dissertations/AAI3704041

Massey, D., & Denton, N. (1993). *American Apartheid: Segregation and the making of the underclass*. Cambridge, MA: Harvard University Press.

Picower, B. (2009). The unexamined Whiteness of teaching: How White teachers maintain and enact dominant racial ideologies. *Race Ethnicity and Education*, *12*(2), 197–215.

Sleeter, C. (2001). Preparing teachers for culturally diverse schools: Research and the overwhelming presence of Whiteness. *Journal of Teacher Education*, *52*(94), 94–106.

Stoudt, B. G., Fine, M., & Fox, M. (2011). Growing up policed in the age of aggressive policing policies. *New York Law School Law Review*, *56*, 1331.

Sue, D. W., Capodilupo, C. M., Torino, G. C., Bucceri, J. M., Holder, A., Nadal, K. L., & Esquilin, M. (2007). Racial microaggressions in everyday life: Implications for clinical practice. *American Psychologist*, *62*(4), 271.

12 Khaki Drag

Race, Gender, and the Performance of Professionalism in Teacher Education

Harper Benjamin Keenan

My alarm goes off at 5:30 a.m. – time to wake up and begin a full day of observations and teaching. I shower and scarf down some oatmeal before the dreaded moment arrives: it is time to face the closet. I pull out a pair of drab, ill-fitting khakis, unbutton a pale blue dress shirt from its hanger, and take out a pair of camel brown leather loafers. I sigh and think, "How utterly boring." You would think that, after coming out as queer as an adolescent, I would have picked up some more creative formalwear, but it is not something I have mastered, especially not in my professional context.

I am a doctoral student working in a teacher education program at an elite university. Here, majestic stone buildings are nestled within carefully landscaped gardens, wine and cheese are served at events about poverty and education, and there is a stable on campus for people to board their horses. Meanwhile, most of the workers who trim the hedges, prepare the wine and cheese, and shovel the horse manure commute from low-income communities across the freeway. It is largely in these neighborhoods that the teacher candidates I work with do their student teaching. For most of the teacher candidates, the majority of whom are White women, these neighborhoods are vastly different from the ones they grew up in.

In many ways, I am a lot like the White students I teach. My choices in clothing are no small part of that. For me, facing the closet every morning is both a literal and symbolic act. As I select clothes to wear in order to be deemed "professional" by my colleagues, so too do I adorn myself with a kind of armor against the imposter syndrome I experience on campus as a queer and transgender person. Drab as they are, these clothes are a costume – its origins rooted in Whiteness and wealth – worn to perform a formal masculinity that is acceptable in my work environment.

In some larger sense, this costuming is a form of drag: a quintessential queer art form that scholar Eve Sedgwick (1993) once aptly described as "kinda subversive, kinda hegemonic" (p. 15). Broadly speaking, "drag," to me, is a conscious performance of identity that refuses to accept its nature as innate (and I should be clear that my knowledge of drag emerges less from queer theory and more out of queer practice). But this drag is not the celebratory, glitter-and-sequins-with-heels-that-could-kill look that the term may conjure for some. The world of *khaki* drag is one drenched in starch. It is a stifling, stiffening, ironing-out of the complex fibers in the fabric that expresses my "outlawed gender" to the world (Bornstein, 2013). It is Clark Kent's gray trench coat and suit worn over Superman's magnificently campy, brightly colored spandex so that he can blend in and access the world of the mundane. It is a costume that reinforces hegemonic notions of manhood and professionalism while my genderqueer body beneath it subverts those norms.

I was not, as Lady Gaga suggests, "born this way." My ability to shift into this performance of bourgeois White masculinity is *not* something that I was born knowing how to do. When I was a kid, I loved dressing up in sneakers, necklaces, sequins, and baseball caps all at once. Over time, through the experience of being immersed in White-dominated familial, social, and institutional contexts, I learned that in order to access power and respect, I was supposed to follow a strict set of rules about what to wear and how to wear it. As a White kid raised in a predominately White community, I learned that Whiteness holds gender normativity as an essential component of its code of "respectability." My experiences as a young trans person taught me that to divert from that code would threaten my safety, and many of those experiences were at school.

Schools reward conformity to Whiteness and binary gender norms at every level from preschool to university. Those of us who diverge from these norms are only deemed acceptable if we dress up to match the school's normative ideals. Of course, elitism requires that not everybody can be accepted as legible in these dress-up clothes. Not everyone can "pass." My university's normative ideals favor people who are White, able-bodied, fluent in "academic" English, cisgender, straight, and wealthy, among many other characteristics. The degree to which a person is successful here depends, in part, on their proximity to each of these categories. Put simply, the terms of the university are these: as long as you look like every other Brooks Brothers bro on campus, you will get along just fine.

It is precisely because of my ability to shift into a legible performance of these normative ideals that I have been granted access to what transgender legal scholar Dean Spade (2010) refers to as the "buffer zone," wherein those of us with divergent bodies and backgrounds are granted access to the university and whose presence is subsequently used to legitimize the myth of meritocracy. Although my trans-ness and queer-ness are identities that diverge from the university's status quo, my White masculinity and access to wealth uphold it.

When I left my job as an elementary school teacher in Brooklyn to pursue a doctorate, I decided that I would be fully out as both queer and transgender. I wanted to work against the trap of allowing the power and advantage of the university to silence parts of who I am. I have sought, with intermittent success, to expose how it is precisely because of my ability to perform the hegemonic elements of khaki drag (read: heteropatriarchal Whiteness), *not* my trans-ness, that I have been let into this elite circle of academia. Making the decision to be out and outspoken has not made my life at university easier. It means uncomfortable stares and inappropriate questions about my body and life from colleagues. It means feeling terribly alone and far from the communities I am closest to, and in which many people are suffering. It means bearing the burden of tokenization by being invited to join one unpaid committee after another, which make claims to diversity and inclusion simply by existing, but maintain top-down organizational structures that typically resist any tangible change.

The challenges that I face in navigating the university intersect with challenges faced by the teacher candidates I work with whose bodies do not fit into normative ideals. Similarly, many of the children that they work with each day also do not fit into normative ideals of what it means to be valuable in society. As much as possible, I try to highlight, decode, and disrupt the reproduction of this phenomenon with the candidates I teach.

At the beginning of every school year, I first attempt this disruption by coming out. I disclose my queer and trans identities to all of the teacher candidates at the beginning of a course I teach called Schooling and Inequity. I do not know how to discuss why and how I think about inequity in schooling without including these parts of who I am. When I come out to the cohort, they witness an educator becoming vulnerable in search of greater connection. It is also a political act in resistance to the ways in which teachers are taught to distance themselves from their own humanity, and to be alienated from that of their students. Central to my philosophy as an educator is that teachers ought to do the things they ask of their students, so it is important to me to model the type of vulnerability with my graduate students that I hope they will embody in their own classrooms. As teacher educator Jonathan Silin (1999) writes, sharing the central parts of who we are is a "matter of integrity" as we implore our students to foster authentic dialogue with children.

As a teacher educator, everything I do is an act of modeling. In all of my teaching, it is crucial that I am just as public in my always-developing analysis of Whiteness and racism as I am about heteropatriarchy and cissexism. As a White queer, it is easy for me to fall into a trap of talking only about the ways I am oppressed and not enough about the privilege I experience. If I do not talk about race and listen carefully to my students' experiences of identity, I risk losing opportunities to support White candidates in developing their racial analysis, and to build an intersectional analysis among all of my students (Crenshaw, 1991).

Last year, I had the opportunity to work alongside teacher candidates in examining how normative ideals manifest in schools. I worked as a first grade mentor teacher in a local summer school program organized through a partnership between the university and a local school district. Returning to the daily practice of teaching children after two years of doctoral coursework gave me the rejuvenating opportunity to sing and play games with six-year-olds while supporting them in learning to read. It also reminded me, in a way that no journal article can, of the challenges and complexities of elementary education.

One of my two student teachers, Peter, had graduated from college less than a month before he entered our graduate program. Warm and enthusiastic, Peter was a young, queer, Black and Chinese-American man that grew up in a nearby community. Peter and I bonded quickly in our first meeting that summer – we buzzed about the upcoming Pride festivities that weekend, and as we got to know each other, we discussed how our students and colleagues might interact with each of our queerness differently given that he was biracial and cisgender, and I was White and trans.

I noted Peter's fresh suede shoes, and he explained that he had just purchased some new professional attire for teaching. At the start of the teacher education program every year, the staff outlines what candidates are expected to wear to their placement schools. Some of the schools that we partner with have strict guidelines for what teachers should and should not wear, and it is our responsibility as teacher educators to be transparent about that. Our candidates need to know what is expected of them in their placements. And yet, when we teach our candidates to unquestioningly accept these expectations as professionalism, we reinforce the power of institutions to regulate the bodies within them.

Dress codes are not new. They emerge from a long tradition of institutional control over which attire is deemed appropriate for teachers and students. Sociologist David L. Brunsma (2004) argues that "the tree of our collective memory in the United States regarding school clothing has its roots planted deeply in British soil" (p. 3) where strict rules for attire were originally used by school authorities to "encourage docility and obedience toward 'rightful authority'" (p. 5) as early as the thirteenth century. This norm became the standard for the United States, where school clothing was similarly used to encourage docility in children, and also to "deculturalize" Native people and other people of Color (Spring, 2001). In other words, the phrase "dress code" is often, quite literally, a code for enforced recognition of the authority of Whiteness and wealth.

Herein lies the hidden curriculum: when we teach teachers that their bodies are only professionally acceptable if they conform to a particular expectation, we reinforce broader societal messages that encourage people to evaluate bodies based on how they look, and we model that this is an acceptable practice for teachers. When we do not examine how those expectations are racialized, gendered, and classed, we implicitly teach that some bodies inherently belong, but others do not. I was confronted by the repercussions of this message last summer.

A few weeks after my initial meeting with Peter, it was the first day of school, and Alex was the first child to arrive. Eagerly, he asked if we had any books about volcanoes (unfortunately, we did not). Out of our 27 students, Alex was the tallest. He was Black and Latino, and the darkest-skinned student among his peers, who were mostly Mexican American, Central American, and South Asian. Like most first graders, he was also learning to tie his shoes. The combination of his untethered laces and high level of energy and excitement meant that he often tripped and bumped into his peers on the way down.

During our first lunch period with the other classes in the cafeteria, Alex got up from his seat to talk to his peers several times, and tripped more than once, resulting in some spilled milk and animal crackers across the floor. This led other teachers to express concern about Alex. One colleague approached me with raised eyebrows and said, "You're really going to have to watch out for that one, huh?" I found this comment disturbing. As anyone who works in a school knows, lunch is notoriously the most hectic time of day, and Alex was not the only child up out of their seat. Why was that a problem? And why were Alex's actions being highlighted in particular? Would the same things have been said if Alex did not have darker skin than his peers? Would they have been said to me if I were not White?

As I walked back to the classroom, I could not shake the feeling that it seemed that Alex's actions were more noticeable and interpreted as problematic because of the ways in which his body – specifically, his height and skin tone – was seen as different from his peers in a school staffed almost entirely by White women. Peter had also noticed and been troubled by the focus on Alex as a problem, but was unsure of what to do. After school, we analyzed the way the racially coded language used to describe Alex could contribute to the construction of a narrow vision for the meaning of Alex's body in the world. We discussed how we could work to resist that by using language to describe Alex's actions in a way that did not characterize him as malicious and that might open more possibility for different meanings of his actions, and how to encourage him to be mindful of his body in space without shaming him. We strategized about how to respond to our colleagues' treatment of Alex in a way that would respectfully challenge the bias we perceived.

Our summer together provided Peter and me with a unique opportunity to build solidarity with each other that would last throughout his time in the program. Over coffee and in impromptu hallway chats, Peter and I talked about our experiences of being different, the pressures and sorrows of feeling alone, and how all of these might shape our teaching practices. Although my role in these conversations was to serve as a mentor to Peter, they also influenced my own pedagogy, and inspired me to cultivate a racially diverse network of queer teachers with whom I can connect queer candidates.

In working with Peter, my life experience was at once beneficial and limiting. I was able to provide one version of critical analysis of schooling, an alternative professional vision, and an example of personal vulnerability in practice. I could connect with him on some of the challenges that arise for queer educators by sharing my perspective as a queer trans person in the highly gendered world of elementary education. Although we could not fully understand each other's individual perspectives and struggles, we were able to listen to each other and be accountable to what we heard.

I was not, however, able to give Peter all of what he needed. I had no experience to offer Peter in how he might relate to Alex or his future students around race, or how to deal with the specific ways that re-entering the public school system might reawaken painful memories of racism for him. Given the personal nature of teaching, candidates need mentors who know something about what it is like to be who they are in a classroom. Peter did not get any opportunities to observe a male teacher of Color that summer, nor were there any men of Color on the staff of our elementary education program for him to talk to.

My summer with Peter and Alex highlighted for me the ways in which the system of schooling attempts to squeeze all of us into boxes we cannot all fit into. By filing away at my queer edges and emphasizing my Whiteness, my performance of khaki drag allows me to pass, but what I have learned is that it does not, on its own, grant access and safety to others to whom passing is not fully available. The phenomenon of passing as a requirement for acceptance inherently means that we leave parts of ourselves behind. It relies on the violent erasure of the full spectrum of humanity. As teacher educators, we must guide our students to build classrooms that create space for children and teachers to explore and express more of who they are, not less.

References

Bornstein, K. (2013). *Gender Outlaw: On men, women and the rest of us.* New York, NY: Routledge.

Brunsma, D. L. (2004). *The School Uniform Movement and What It Tells Us about American Education: A symbolic crusade.* Lanham, MD: Scarecrow Education.

Crenshaw, K. (1991). Mapping the margins: Intersectionality, identity politics, and violence against women of color. *Stanford Law Review, 43*(6), 1241–1299.

Sedgwick, E. K. (1993). Queer performativity: Henry James's the art of the novel. *GLQ: A Journal of Lesbian and Gay Studies, 1*(1), 1–16.

Silin, J. G. (1999). Teaching as a gay man: Pedagogical resistance or public spectacle? *GLQ: A Journal of Lesbian and Gay Studies, 5*(1), 95–106.

Spade, D. (2010). Be Professional! *Harvard Journal of Law and Gender, 33*(71), 1–12.

Spring, J. H. (2001). *Deculturalization and the Struggle for Equality: A brief history of the education of dominated cultures in the United States.* Boston, MA: McGraw-Hill.

13 "Democratic" for Whom?

Teaching Racial Justice through Critical Pedagogy

Joanne Tien

[handwritten margin note: I made [?] if we approach each other from a standpoint of theoretical respect, world would be different]

It was the fourth week of class, and I had shown a YouTube clip from the movie *Crash*. In the clip, two Black men who attend UCLA notice how a wealthy White woman passing by immediately clung tighter to her husband's arm upon approaching them. Though I was using this movie clip as a tool to get students to think about how our personal experiences and social positioning influence our construction of knowledge, students were more immediately struck by the incident of racial profiling portrayed in the movie.

Darby,[1] an Asian American woman, commented: "I definitely agree knowledge is situated, not objective... In this case, it's called profiling... I think it's something really understandable, but I think it's really not correct. We shouldn't judge people based on their race, but it's really hard not to."

Sheila, a White woman, then added: "I agree we should never judge people at all, but it's really hard when you're in a situation... fear overtakes judgement. My first day here, I lived really far from campus and I never felt safe, and it was justified... It's a weird hypocrisy because it's a fact that in certain situations it is dangerous."

Following her comment, the room tensed over. I could see the discomfort on the faces of Black and Brown students in the class, and I myself felt angry by what sounded like a justification of racial profiling based on the students' experiences with feeling "unsafe" in "certain neighborhoods."

Critical Pedagogy and its Internal Contradictions

This scenario illustrates some of the tensions teacher educators face in addressing racial justice in the classroom. As a teacher educator invested in the use of critical pedagogy, I have found it particularly difficult to navigate two seemingly contradictory goals within its practice. On the one hand, in order to avoid "banking" or depositing knowledge into my students in an authoritarian manner, I use a democratic, constructivist approach, encouraging students to construct knowledge from their own experiences. At the same time, however, I also want my students to develop an explicit critique of the social order that is antiracist, antisexist, and anticapitalist

(Freire, 1998). This leaves me with a dilemma: what happens if students' experiences don't lead them to conclusions that challenge oppression?

This chapter will address this paradox by exploring my experiences as a queer Asian American activist-educator using critical pedagogy to teach racial justice in a classroom comprised mostly of White and Asian American teacher education students at an elite public university. Drawing from Paulo Freire's (1970) theory of critical pedagogy, ED280: Democratic Learning and Critical Education seeks to foster "the awakening of critical awareness" (p. 19) and "the action and reflection of men and women upon their world in order to transform it" (p. 79). Students in ED280 examine the reproduction of structural inequality through schooling, race, class, gender, ethnicity, ideology, and culture. The course also draws from the liberal Deweyan ideal of school as an "embryonic community," wherein all members feel validated as equal participants in the classroom (Dewey, 1899). Designed to attract future teachers, ED280 also requires students to examine their own positionalities within larger systems of power (focusing primarily on race, class, and gender). Thus, as the instructor of the class, I must navigate the inherent contradictions within critical pedagogy. Because students enter the classroom as racialized and gendered subjects, there is no such thing as a truly non-hierarchical space. At the same time, critical pedagogy aims to create such a democratic space, while simultaneously leading students to an explicit critique of the social order.

Thus, I interrogate how my positionality impacts the extent to which I am able to facilitate equal representation of voices – or make decisions about when some experiences should be highlighted over others. I find that my identification with race as a *political* construction opens new possibilities both for relating to students, and for students to see themselves as agents of social change. In so doing, I argue that educators' ability to create "democratic" classroom spaces is always mediated by relations of power within the larger sociopolitical context.

Negotiating Positionality

Through my teaching, I have found that it is in the negotiation of positionality – of both students and teacher – that the tension between democratic learning and antiracist education is most clearly illuminated. As an Asian American person, I accrue some benefits from White supremacy due to my racial identity being valorized relative to White and Black people (Kim, 1999). At the same time, however, I am positioned as an "outsider-within," having "inside" knowledge of White power, yet always situated as an "outsider" within White institutions (Hill Collins, 2000). Though this experience of racial triangulation has always made me feel alienated from American society, it has also given me the privilege of accessing higher education despite coming from a working class family. Growing up in a conservative Christian household, my struggle to come to terms with my queerness and gender fluid identity also exacerbated my feelings of alienation. As a result of embodying multiple subjectivities (Anzaldúa, 1987; Cruz, 2001), my personal process of identity development mirrored my political development as a leftist, feminist, and antiracist educator.

These experiences significantly inform my teaching. They enable me to empathize with the various and multiple subjectivities from which my students enter the classroom, and remind me that both ideology and identity are unstable and constantly under production (Hall, 1990). This recognition helps me prioritize the creation of a democratic classroom that draws from students' experiences. At the same time, however, because my racial identity intersects with a marginalized class and gender identity, my life experiences have also taught me that education is always political (Apple, 1990), and a liberatory education must side with the oppressed (Freire, 1970).

Tensions in the Classroom

While aligning well with the principles of critical pedagogy, these dual convictions − of forefronting student experiences and teaching explicitly anti-oppressive curricula − often lead to paradoxical teaching dilemmas. The anecdote above illustrates just one. In this scenario, Sheila, a White woman, drew from her own personal experiences and came to the conclusion that racial profiling is justified and necessary for protecting her own safety. This comment in turn created a hostile space for Black and Brown students in the class who *have* been racially profiled, and continue to be profiled on a regular basis at an elite campus like our own. I worried that our emphasis on "democracy" in the classroom had in reality created a "safe" space for maintaining White comfort at the expense of symbolic violence against Black and Brown students (Leonardo & Porter, 2010). Such violence is often unrecognizable in that it appears "natural" as part of the daily functioning of social life. ~~But it's not~~

This led me to a pedagogical dilemma. On the one hand, I could interrogate Sheila's experiences with the hopes that through such engagement, she would come to see her validation of racial profiling as rooted in a particular raced, classed, and gendered worldview. In so doing, however, I would be centering White experience within the classroom discussion, at the expense of the learning of Black and Brown students who did not need a lesson on racial profiling. Worse, in centering White experience, I could also unintentionally create a dynamic whereby Black and Brown students feel obligated to "teach" their peers about their experiences with racism.

On the other hand, I could move on with the class discussion, which was intended to examine how our experiences and social positioning affect our construction of knowledge. Given that most classes in the university already cater to the experiences of White students, I chose this latter option because I felt that it was more important to prioritize the learning of students of Color in this situation. I also did not want to stretch the meaning of

requires wisdom and courage!

"democracy" such that it became acceptable to make racist statements in our classroom. In later reflecting upon this scenario, however, I realized that in the interest of de-centering whiteness, I had chosen not to acknowledge the White student's experiences at all, ironically, on the same day that we were discussing how personal experiences can be a source of knowledge. In so doing, I forfeited a potentially fruitful discussion that may have enabled the student and her peers to think more critically about the racial structuring of the social order. Furthermore, I potentially silenced the White student from freely sharing her experiences in the future. *Not good either because this person's personal experience was also real.*

Democratic Learning and Antiracist Education

Freirean and feminist scholars have argued that personal experience is key to the development of knowledge and truth: it is only when students feel their voices valued that shifts in racial ideology can occur. At the same time, however, Kathleen Weiler (1991) has noted that "there are contradictions involved in claiming that... emotions are a source for knowledge and at the same time arguing that they are manipulated and shaped by dominant discourses" (p. 463). The same could be said for experience. Though Sheila, the White student, was right in drawing from her experiences to observe that women are often the victims of violence in a patriarchal society, she still failed to see how her experiences led her to a truth that was partial. In constructing knowledge from her own experiences without taking into account how they have been shaped by the dominant racial ideologies of our society, Sheila came to the racialized conclusion that dark-skinned people are the primary source of violence against women. *The power of word and media.* For me, this scenario is a useful reminder that our experiences are always mediated by the dominant social order. As Freirean teacher educators, we must avoid falling into the trap of allowing our emphasis on student experience to become a form of "individual therapy" (Weiler, 1991) that validates White comfort and safety (Leonardo & Porter, 2010). Rather, we must recognize the classroom as a site of contestation and struggle, and learn to *challenge*, rather than *silence* dominant discourses. Moreover, we must teach our students to do the same.

Antiracist Curricula as a Tool for Social Transformation

Though it may seem to contradict the principles of democratic education, I have found that centering explicitly antiracist curricula over individual student experiences can open new possibilities both for relating to students and for students to see themselves as agents of social change. In fact, race is the central organizing principle of my syllabus for a course on democratic education. I do this because I have found that there is no such thing as a truly democratic or non-hierarchical space in a world structured by racial oppression (Smith, 2013). Because the production of space is already political, space is never neutral, but rather a manifestation of camouflaged power structures (Foucault & Miskowiec, 1986). Thus, in centering antiracist curricula over experiential learning, I aim to create a more democratic space by illuminating these camouflaged power structures. This in turn will make for the development of future teachers who are prepared to construct a more democratic society.

In explicitly teaching antiracist curricula, White students in my class were able to understand how race is socially constructed. This in turn enabled them to transcend "White guilt" (Katz, 1978/2003) and recognize that they have agency in acting against whiteness. For example, in reflecting on Tomás Almaguer's (2008) study of racial formation, *Racial Fault Lines*, Sheila was able to observe that "the root... of racial discrimination lies in the race for control over land and the capitalist market" and "since being categorized in a certain 'race' determined one's financial and political status, the closer one was labeled to being 'White' the better access to opportunities of advancement they had." From this observation, Sheila also thoughtfully reflected on her own positionality, writing:

> I realized that... White people are able to recognize their privileges... and as a result of that it is possible to collectively change the social order. Because in this case, the people of Color are not playing catch-up with the Whites, but rather the Whites work to give up, or equalize, "privileges"... [This] is the tool to actually changing racial discrimination in America.

This quote represents a shift in Sheila's consciousness from the beginning of the semester, when the *Crash* incident had occurred. Rather than defending the racial order, Sheila now felt moved to challenge it.

In centering antiracist curricula, this course also created a space for non-White students to reflect upon their own experiences as racialized subjects and understand the historical and political importance of their racial identities. In a course reflection, one student wrote:

> I never saw myself as oppressed, even as an Asian, Female, [and] American Alien who came from a colonized country, and struggled with hidden disabilities... learning about oppression... [gave me a] sudden revelation... I had not realized the deep rooted effects of colonialism until that very day.

Students of Color were also given space to interrogate the effects of internalized racism and colonialism in their own lives. In another reflection, a student wrote that this process enabled her to become "more critical of present-day institutions... and feel that I have more of a sense of responsibility to change the oppressive environment I am in." For students who were already familiar with issues of racial justice, this class affirmed their racial identities and empowered them to be involved in movements for social change. At the end of the semester, several students of Color commented on how this class had helped them understand education as activism, and teaching as a form of organizing. Very different from chapter 11

Finally, for many students, this class was also a unique space to explore their identities as Asian American women. This occurred not because we shared a cultural or ethnic heritage, but because we shared common experiences of oppression and political vision. In fact, assumptions of cultural homogeneity or claims to cultural authenticity tended to further alienate students who did not feel that they fit within any prescribed social category. As Du Bois (1940/1996) has argued, when it comes to race, "the physical bond is least and the badge of color relatively unimportant save as a badge; the real essence of... kinship... is its social heritage... the discrimination and insult" (p. 640). It is this understanding of race as political that enables me to relate to students across racial difference and empower them to become agents for social change.

In developing their "critical consciousness" through this course, both White students and students of Color are now better prepared to become teachers who challenge racism in their classrooms and provoke social change at their school sites. Students frequently note that this course has inspired them to speak out against authority. Similarly, White students have commented that they are no longer able to have conversations with their family members and peers without feeling the need to interrupt coded "colorblind" language, while students of Color often identify more strongly with their racial backgrounds. These changes are transformative in preparing future teachers who will be able to interrupt racial violence in their classrooms and create spaces that affirm their students' racial identities.

Conclusion

The true challenge for future educators today is to learn how to navigate democratic teaching in an undemocratic society, already structured by centuries of racial oppression. In teaching ED280: Democratic Learning and Critical Education, I have realized that negotiating between democratic learning, antiracist objectives, and teacher/student positionalities requires constant navigation. While there is no formula for how to do this, our work is to develop critical teachers who can make strategic decisions to highlight the voices of students of Color, even at the cost of failing to create a "non-hierarchical" classroom or de-centering White experience. Our public schools need educators who can acknowledge the ways by which the presumed "equality" of the student voice is already mediated by racialized structures. Future educators must *challenge* rather than *silence* dominant discourses, for only in so doing can racialized ideologies be exposed. Moreover, in uplifting race as *political*, rather than cultural or biological, future teachers can build relationships with students across racial difference, while empowering students to see themselves as agents of social change. Through navigating the classroom as a site of struggle, critical educators might fulfill Freire's (1970) vision of education as "the practice of freedom."

Note

1 Names have been changed.

References

Almaguer, T. (2008). *Racial Fault Lines: The historical origins of White Supremacy in California*. Berkeley, CA: University of California Press.

Anzaldúa, G. (1987). *Borderlands/La frontera: The new mestiza*. San Francisco, CA: Aunt Lute.

Apple, M. W. (1990). *Ideology and Curriculum*. New York, NY: Routledge.

Cruz, C. (2001). Toward an epistemology of the brown body. *Qualitative Studies in Education 14*(5), 657–669.

Dewey, J. (1899). *The School and Society: Being three lectures*. New York, NY: McClure, Phillips & Company.

Du Bois, W. E. B. (1996). Dusk of dawn: An essay toward an autobiography of a race concept. In N. Huggins (Ed.), *Writings* (pp. 551–1325). New York, NY: Library of America (Original work published in 1940).

Foucault, M., & Miskowiec, J. (1986). Of other spaces. *Diacritics, 16*(1), 22–27.

Freire, P. (1970). *Pedagogy of the Oppressed*. New York, NY: Continuum International Publishing Group, Inc.

Freire, P. (1998). *Pedagogy of Freedom: Ethics, democracy, and civic courage*. Lanham, MD: Rowman & Littlefield.

Hall, S. (1990). Cultural identity and diaspora. In J. Rutherford (Ed.), *Identity: Community, culture, difference* (pp. 222–237). London, UK: Lawrence & Wishart.

Hill Collins, P. (2000). *Black Feminist Thought: Knowledge, consciousness, and the politics of empowerment*. New York, NY: Routledge.

Katz, J. (2003). *White Awareness: Handbook for anti-racism training*. Oklahoma, OK: University of Oklahoma Press (Original work published 1978).

Kim, E. (1999). The racial triangulation of Asian Americans. *Politics and Society, 27*(1), 105–138.

Leonardo, Z., & Porter, R. (2010). Pedagogy of fear: Toward a Fanonian theory of 'safety' in race dialogue. *Race, Ethnicity, and Education, 13*(2), 139–157.

Smith, A. (2013). Unsettling the privilege of self-reflexivity. In F. W. Twine & B. Gardener (Eds.), *Geographies of Privilege* (pp. 263–280). New York, NY: Routledge.

Weiler, K. (1991). Freire and a feminist pedagogy of difference. *Harvard Educational Review, 61*(4), 449–474.

14 Solidarity as ~~Praxis~~ formal Praxis

Injury, Ethics, and Hope in Teacher Education

Sameena Eidoo

I began thinking about possibilities of solidarity in and through anti-oppressive praxis in preservice teacher education during my first post-doctoral teaching assignment at a faculty of education in Toronto, Canada. I was responsible for teaching multiple sections of a foundational course that critically examines the relationship between school and society, beginning with a cohort of teacher candidates (hereafter referred to as "candidates") interested in teaching and learning in urban schools.

Among the candidates in the first cohort was Iman, a young Muslim woman of Colour. Iman was engaged in intentional political projects in local communities. With a lack of critical content, she was experiencing the program as oppressive, and sometimes disengaged as a strategy to preserve her well-being. The first few classes – a series of assigned texts focusing on pedagogies of the city: the construction of "urban–suburban" dichotomy, gentrification and the racialization of space in the Greater Toronto Area (GTA) (Daniel, 2010) – generated anger among some candidates, which spilled over from the classroom to the online discussion forum. Iman approached me to check in with me to make sure I was okay, to discuss what had happened, and to provide some background information about the cohort to help me contextualize the situation. I recall feeling apprehensive about accepting her support, because I was "the teacher" and she was "the student." But, I acquiesced because I needed support. I implicitly trusted Iman.

Iman committed to participating actively in classroom discussion, compassionately interrupting and challenging oppressive discourses circulating among fellow candidates. She served as a witness to microaggressions and aggressions. Iman encouraged me to continue engaging in anti-oppressive praxis. In our encounter, we met somewhere halfway, as teacher–student power relations inversed from asymmetrical to symmetrical. The following passage in Paulo Freire's seminal work *Pedagogy of the Oppressed* (1970) comes close to capturing this relational shift:

> Through dialogue, the teacher-of-the-students and the students-of-the-teacher cease to exist and a new term emerges: teacher–student with students–teachers. The teacher is no longer merely the-one-who-teaches,

but one who is [herself] taught in dialogue with the students, who in turn while being taught also teach. They become jointly responsible for a process in which all grow.

(p. 80)

Iman and I discussed how to engage in anti-oppressive praxis amid often overwhelming resistance. We worked conscientiously and strategically with and for each other. As Freire (1970) writes,

> Solidarity requires that one enter into the situation of those with whom one is in solidarity; it is a radical posture… True solidarity with the oppressed means fighting at their side to transform the objective reality, which has made them these "beings for one another."

(p. 49)

For Freire solidarity entails the acknowledgement of liberation as a collective project requiring dialogic teaching, learning, and critical consciousness of the ties that bind the oppressor and the oppressed together. Iman and I were both experiencing the classroom environment as oppressive, and we became "beings for one another." While I learned from all of the candidates in the cohort, my encounter with Iman transformed my understanding of the teacher–student dichotomy, and created new possibilities for solidarity.

In the following pages, I reflect on the nature and meaning of such beautiful encounters of solidarity I have had the privilege of witnessing and experiencing through my work as a teacher educator.

Where I Am From

I am the Canada-born daughter of Muslim parents who migrated from India in the late 1960s and early 1970s. I am the first in my immediate family to enter the educational system in Canada. I grew up in a mixed income neighbourhood in the GTA. I attended elementary, middle, and secondary school in the same neighbourhood where I lived. I attended elementary school at a time when each day began with the collective singing of the National Anthem *and* the communal recitation of the Lord's Prayer.[1] I still know the Lord's Prayer by heart. A portrait of Queen Elizabeth II hung in the front foyer of the school.

For a brief while, my mother volunteered at the elementary school as a translator for Urdu and Hindi-speaking children and families. I loved when my mother visited the school. I attended Islamic school at the weekends. At home, I had access to Urdu, Arabic, and English texts. I began to speak less Urdu and more English, and became separated from my home language and culture as I progressed steadily through the K-12 educational system. These are among the early experiences of schooling, experiences I carry with me into my work in preservice teacher education. Unlearning internalized oppression is part of my ongoing work. The intellectual and affective labour of critical educational scholar activists unapologetically committed to anti-oppressive praxis holds me up.

As a teacher educator, I have strived to serve children, youth, and families underserved or pushed out by the K-12 public educational system. They are part of my "community of accountability," and a source of courage I draw from to engage in anti-oppressive praxis in teacher education. I believe teacher education is a critical site for disrupting oppressive discourses and practices candidates may bring with them into the program and take with them into classrooms, schools, and communities.

I am self-consciously aware I am a "body out of place," in Canadian schools and society. As Sarah Ahmed (2000) observes, "The stranger is not any-body that we have failed to recognize, but some-body that we have already recognized as a stranger, as 'a body out of place'" (p. 55). Within settler colonial states like Canada and the United States, the Indigenous and people of Colour are already recognized as "strangers": "While the Indigenous 'Other' represents the strangeness of the disappearing/disappeared state of nature, the Brown/Black diasporic 'Other' represents the strangeness of immanent danger and the prospect of terror. Both are denied subjectivity, yet neither can claim innocence" (Gaztambide-Fernádez, 2012, p. 20).

Teacher Educator/Muslim Woman of Colour

Six months after my course with Iman, I began another set of foundation courses, including a cohort of approximately 70 candidates, predominately White, preparing to teach in Catholic elementary and secondary schools. I was surprised by the assignment, because I had no prior experience of Catholic education. I later learned the assignment was "deliberate" – an effort to provide those candidates with the opportunity to learn from an educator they would not likely experience otherwise. Ontario Catholic school boards[2] will only consider applications from prospective teachers who are Catholic, and prospective teachers must submit a reference from their parish priest as part of the application process. Despite my concerns about my lack of experience in Catholic education and how candidates might receive my presence and teaching as a Muslim woman of Colour, I approached my work with an open mind, heart, and spirit. I had recently taught a graduate-level seminar on the life and work of Freire, whose praxis was informed by liberation theology.

Classes began the week of September 11. I was compelled to engage candidates in pedagogical dilemmas of teaching in a post-9/11 era, and thereby to introduce candidates to my teaching philosophy, commitments, and self. I invited candidates to reflect on where they were on 9/11, how they had learned about what had happened, whether any of their K-12 teachers had addressed 9/11 in the classroom, and whether they would address 9/11 in their own classrooms and how. Amber, a young woman with an Arab father, shared she had been subject to Islamophobic and racist bullying by peers at the Ontario Catholic elementary school she had attended. They questioned whether her father had flown an airplane into one of the Twin Towers in New York City. She shared she had never before shared the story publicly, and she felt the same hurt and anger she had experienced as an elementary school student well up when she shared her story.

After some further discussion, I invited candidates to take turns reading aloud from *This is Where I Need to Be* (2008) a volume of oral histories collected by and for Muslim youth living in New York City in the immediate aftermath of 9/11. As the introduction states,

> From the very beginning, students wanted to do more than write oral histories that would simply respond to negative perceptions of Muslims. Alongside stories of discrimination and pain, they collected stories that spoke to the desires, beauty and humor in the lives of Muslim youth in New York City.

> (p. iv)

I wanted to fill the classroom with this knowledge and experience in an effort to counter deficit storytelling and to amplify stories hardly told or heard in classrooms. A growing number of Ontario Catholic school boards are admitting students from all faith communities, and therefore candidates interested in Catholic education must be prepared to support students and families from all faith communities, including Muslims. I closed the class with a live recording of Palestinian poet Suheir Hammad's performance of *First Writing Since*, a poem she had revised in response to the aftermath of 9/11 and read for her brothers. The poem refutes post-9/11 Islamophobic and anti-Arab discourses and practices.

Solidarity as Praxis: Inside the Classroom

At the end of the first class, several candidates stayed behind to speak with me one-to-one, to continue the discussion I had initiated in class, to share their excitement about the learning experiences they had just had and the learning opportunities they anticipated, and to affirm that my presence and teaching was needed in the cohort. Through such initial and subsequent interactions with candidates, I learned my course content was distinct relative to their other courses in the following ways: it focused on anti-oppressive theory and practice in and through education; and it required reading and listening to different kinds of texts centring the experiential knowledge of students and families from historically and presently marginalized communities in Canadian schools and society. My pedagogical approach was different in the following ways: it de-centred whiteness; it required candidates to demonstrate understanding of their positionality and its implications for their interactions with texts and others, particularly the children, families, and communities their schools were supposed to serve; and it called on candidates to use experiences of discomfort in the classroom to expand and deepen self-understanding. Some candidates felt a sense of connection to my teaching and presence. For other candidates, particularly those with internalized dominance accustomed to learning environments structured for their comfort and those with internalized oppression, my teaching and presence was unsettling.

Among the candidates who approached me after the first class was Tatiana, an Afro-Caribbean young woman and one of two Black candidates in the cohort. During our first conversation, Tatiana and I learned that we shared community connections. She shared that she had been raised Catholic, but felt conflicted about teaching in Catholic schools. She questioned whether anti-oppressive praxis within the existing Catholic educational system was possible. As one of the very few candidates in the cohort with a strong anti-oppressive analysis, Tatiana was often confounded by what she perceived as her peers' wilful and aggressive ignorance. In the second class, for example, the same series of assigned texts focusing on the construction of "urban–suburban" dichotomy, gentrification, and the racialization of space in Canada (Daniel, 2010), generated responses ranging from apathy to anger among some White candidates. Tatiana was upset after that class. She had volunteered to facilitate a small-group discussion, and was stunned by her peers' disengagement with a documentary focusing on youth tenants' experiences of displacement due to gentrification in the GTA. These were youth with whom Tatiana identified as part of her community of accountability.

In the third class, which focused on access to education for undocumented children and youth in Ontario, it took a great deal of work to keep most candidates focused on issues of educational access, rather than expressing often xenophobic opinions on citizenship and immigration. Amber challenged a fellow candidate, an older White man, who was using xenophobic language to discuss undocumented migrants. When I intervened, however, there was an outburst among some other White men demanding I let the older White man speak. I stayed focused on creating space for Amber to say what she needed to say. Amber informed him she felt offended by his language, and her father had been an undocumented migrant. By doing this, Amber also helped create space for another fellow candidate, who approached me after class to share her father had been an undocumented migrant from Cuba, and her family had lived in fear that he would be deported for many years. Prior to this class, she did not know the Ontario Education Act includes provisions for the right to education of children of undocumented migrants. Although I received apologies from the White men who had interrupted, I left the class feeling sick and uneasy about returning.

Amber later confided she wished she had not said anything. She felt responsible for creating conflict within the cohort. Although the classroom climate was palpably different after that class, it was not because Amber spoke out. As the course progressed, and delved further into theory and practice of anti-oppressive education, some older White men in the cohort became increasingly volatile.

After the sixth class, which focused explicitly on race and racism, including racism as White supremacy and antiBlack racism, Tatiana informed me that she had recorded her peers' comments in a notebook and on her phone "just in case" the candidates tried to have me disciplined. I was astounded by her bold actions, foresight, and act of solidarity. Tatiana understood my vulnerability, as well as the power of White candidates' complaints in institutions designed to protect whiteness and structured for their comfort. After that same class, other older White men harassed me.

Tatiana would often stay after class to share her experiences within the cohort, and to reflect on what it might mean to work in Catholic schools. At one point, early in the semester, I asked if she would consider transferring into a different cohort. Despite her frustrations, she insisted on staying. She told me she wanted to be there for me, to support me in educating her peers. Tatiana would often participate actively in small-group and whole-class discussions, refuting oppressive discourses circulating among candidates, particularly racist, classist, and xenophobic discourses. I was awed and humbled by Tatiana's sense of responsibility toward me and her peers, and I committed to continue the work for and with her despite the hostility.

The time and space provided by the winter break did not resolve the tension. Amber approached me with another candidate, Michaela, a biracial young woman, to inform me about what was happening in the cohort. I was stunned and sickened by their allegations of fellow candidates' misconduct, including alleged racist and misogynist comments and actions directed toward me, and an organized effort to have me disciplined for my antiracist teachings. Like Tatiana, they had been documenting fellow candidates' comments and activities, both in person and online. Amber and Michaela went directly to administration to hold those candidates involved accountable. They followed up with a letter to administration, as well as photographic and written documentation of candidates' alleged misconduct, and its impact on their learning and well-being. I recall sitting in my office with Amber and Michaela, listening to them again in awe.

Tatiana, Amber, and Michaela were experiencing and witnessing the same violence, but they wanted me to continue doing the work and they committed to doing the work in solidarity with me.

Solidarity as Praxis: Outside of the Classroom

By the end of the first semester and the beginning of the second semester of that academic year, I had resolved to create a supportive space for candidates of Colour to connect, share, and learn with one another. I wanted to create a protected space in which they could have reprieve from the White gaze and discursive violence often perpetuated by antiracism education in settings dominated by White and middle-class students, and in which their interests could be foregrounded in a predominantly White faculty of education. Initially, there was some backlash. Amber,[3] Michaela, and Tatiana had been approached by a group of White candidates and asked if they were part of "Sameena's secret group," even though fellow faculty were involved in outreach efforts and information about the space was posted throughout the Faculty of Education building. It was no "secret."

The first meeting drew candidates from diverse racial, ethnic, and cultural groups. Some candidates who attended were not entirely certain whether they could or should identify as "people of Colour," while others were fully affirmed in their self-identification as "people of Colour" and had been seeking such a space from the beginning of the academic year. Some candidates attended consistently, while others dropped in on an as-needed basis. Many candidates had encouraged others to attend or took it upon themselves to educate both White candidates and candidates of Colour about the importance of having a space exclusively for candidates who identify as "people of Colour."

Within the space, candidates made connections with one another; exchanged self-care and community-care strategies; practiced caring for themselves and for one another; worked through experiences of racism and strived to unlearn internalized racism; shared teaching and learning resources and strategies; discussed collaborative and coercive interactions with faculty, associate teachers, peers, and students; and prepared for the job search and interview process. The space centralized the knowledge and lived experiences of candidates of Colour, and supported them as they navigated preservice teacher education and the K-12 educational system as future teachers.

Conclusion

As a teacher educator, I have been subject to hostile looks; racist and misogynist comments, threats, and bullying; and various other attempts to discipline me or have me disciplined. I have been concerned for the safety and well-being of candidates witnessing and experiencing peer aggression, and of children and youth who might be placed in classrooms with those candidates. My story is not unique among minoritized faculty engaged in racial justice work, particularly in predominately White universities (e.g. Gutiérrez y Muhs, Niemann, González, & Harris, 2012; Tuck, Carroll, & Smith, 2010). Our stories are counterstories, providing insight into our work and issues of workplace safety. Iman, Tatiana, Amber, and Michaela's solidarity sustained and inspired me. I hope the examples of solidarity shared in this chapter offer insight into relational encounters possible in and through anti-oppressive praxis in teacher education.

Notes

1 In 1988, the Ontario Court of Appeal ruled that use of the Lord's Prayer in opening exercises in public schools offended the Canadian Charter of Rights and Freedoms.
2 In Canada, the K-12 Catholic educational system is a separate one that has constitutional status in three provinces (Alberta, Ontario, and Saskatchewan) and statutory status in three territories (Northwest Territories, Nunavut, and Yukon). Canada's separate school system has been condemned by international human rights bodies. On 5 November 1999, the United Nations Human Rights committee condemned Canada and Ontario for having violated equity provisions of the International Covenant on Civil Rights, and restated/its concerns on 2 November 2005 on the grounds that Canada had failed to "adopt steps in order to eliminate discrimination on the basis of religion in the funding of schools in Ontario." Beyond the funding issue, Canadian Catholic education has been criticized for enabling "religiously-inspired hetero-sexist oppression in school settings" (Callaghan, 2014, p. 223).
3 This group of White candidates read Amber as a person of Colour. Amber self-identified as "White."

References

Ahmed, S. (2000). *Strange Encounters: Embodied others in post-coloniality*. New York, NY: Routledge.

Callaghan, T. D. (2014). My real "gay agenda": Exposing holy homophobia of Catholic schools. In G. Walton (Ed.), *The Gay Agenda: Claiming space, identity and justice* (pp. 223–238). New York, NY: Peter Lang Publishing.

Freire, P. (1970). *Pedagogy of the Oppressed*. New York, NY: Continuum.

Gaztambide-Fernández, R. A. (2012). Decolonization and the pedagogy of solidarity. *Decolonization: Indigeneity, Education and Society, 1*(1), 41–67.

Gutiérrez y Muhs, G., Niemann, Y. F., González, C. G., & Harris, A. P. (Eds.) (2012). *Presumed Incompetent: The intersections of race and class for women in academia*. Boulder, CO: University Press of Colorado.

Tuck, E., Carroll, K. K., & Smith, M. D. (2010). About us and not about us: Theorizing student resistance to race and racism from underrepresented faculty. *Journal of the International Society for Teacher Education, 14*(2), 70–74.

15 "Ew, Why Are You Wearing a Pink Shirt, Mister?"

How a Kindergartner Led Me to Complicate Racial Justice Teaching

Eduardo Lara

soy Nepantlero (i am a Nepantlero) – i exist in between worlds.

before spring break, i introduced a bright, inquisitive Chicana student to Anzaldúa's work, La Frontera/Borderlands, during office hours. i advised her to read it so she can use some of the ideas in the book to write her paper on gender and carwasheros (carwash workers). she read the book i lent her over spring break and even shared the spanish passages with her mom, inspiring an organic pedagogy of the home to transpire between Madre e Hija (Mother and Daughter). beautiful.

she returned the book to me today expressing that she was gonna buy her own copy. i returned it right back to her as a gift and let her know that i have another copy at home and my partner has a copy, so really, i am a walking Anzaldúa library. i hand out books as if i were a paletero (ice cream vendor). con campanas y todo – ¡libros, libros! (with bells and everything – books, books!)

immediately after our meeting, i walked over to the student union for lunch and ran into Chicano parents congregating for their own lonche (lunch). i couldn't just ignore raza (fellow people) that looked like my parents, tios, tias, abuelitos y abuelitas (uncles, aunts, grandpas and grandmas), especially because i've never seen a critical mass of Brown parents on campus before.

"buenas tardes! como estan? bienvenidos a lon bich!..." y asi empezamos a platicar. ("good afternoon! how are you? welcome to long beach..." and that's how we started to chat it up.) turns out they were parents from a migrant family education program that provides info on college access. i gave them my contact info should they ever need help on campus.

i returned to my office to find another student, this time of the horchata variety (white student), waiting for me with a look i am too familiar with – the look of a student that communicates, oh shit, i'm about to come out. indeed, what transpired were heartfelt words acknowledging his sexuality and confiding with me the challenges of being gay. i made sure to let the student know that he's normal and assured him of the safe space he has with me.

Nepantla: the in-between. Queer. Brown. Chicano feminist. all helping me be a better educator. outside the classroom, inside, and in between.

(Social Media Post, April 9, 2014[1])

I share the social media post reflected in the vignette to saliently convey my approach toward antiracist education using a more creative take on writing. The vignette also articulates my positionality as a Queer Chicano, a hybridity of identities that not only occupies the intersection of race, gender, and sexuality, but is also situated in what Anzaldúa (1987) identifies as Nepantla – living in the "in between." I wrote the social media post after an enriching day of teaching, having come across various serendipitous moments when my Queer Chicano educator identity aligned with the particular needs of each situation. My ability to glean from raced, gendered, and sexed experiential knowledge, coupled with my 12 years' experience as a teacher educator, allowed me to respond to these situations in ways that are informed by the intersectional and Nepantla space my identity occupies. The vignette I shared begins to illustrate both the importance of and practices employed when tapping into this conceptual space.

To fully understand the scope of this chapter as a contribution toward paving the way for more diversity that is inclusive of sexuality, I anchor this work with this central question: How do my teaching experiences as a Queer Chicano inform racial justice in teacher education? In addition to the shared vignette, reflecting on this question brings to mind a specific moment that occurred early in my teacher education career when I supervised a second language development (SLD) clinic at a university-partner elementary school. On that day, I wore a stylish pink shirt I was particularly fond of because it embedded some elements of a *guayabera*[2] with a floral design. Walking on to the campus of the school, in my own queer mind, I imagined I was more of a fashionista running down the runway than a teacher education professor. As soon as I walked into the kindergartner classroom to begin my observations of student teachers practicing their sheltered instruction, one of the inquisitive five-year-olds was quick to chop down my runway aspirations by exclaiming, "Ew, why are you wearing a pink shirt, mister?"

SWOOSH!!! Think, record scratches and all eyes are on the DJ. Within seconds, this cute five-year-old commanded a room full of other inquisitive kindergartners and preservice teachers to zoom their attention on to me as I sashayed through the room attempting to jot down observations of the lesson. It was pointless to continue observing lessons, because all eyes were on me and my snazzy pink shirt while the rambunctious kindergartner who should have been paying attention to the lesson, but instead continued, "Pink is for girls!"

I have to admit, in that moment, I exerted great discipline over my facial muscles because I really wanted to laugh due to the charismatic nature of this little boy who commanded the attention of the entire room. My critical lens though, immediately framed the interaction as a gendered microaggression and my repertoire to turn situations like these into a learning moment guided my handling of the interruption. Without skipping a beat, I simply replied to the future Disney star, "Boys can wear pink too. Pink's a cool color!"

Admittedly, my remark was as much a message to the boy as it was to the rest of the impressionable kindergartners. Reflecting back, I was also modeling to my preservice teachers how to turn a classroom interruption into a teaching moment – well, THAT and how to rock a pink shirt with ruffled flowers made out of fabric that popped out from the sleeves. I was tempted to give a twirl in my pink shirt, but instead figured that might be over the top for an after-school SLD clinic. So I just twirled in my head as I exited the room to observe my next round of lessons.

I wish I could say that my handling of the learning moment paid immediate dividends, but I must be candid in the way this particular narrative from my trove of teaching stories ended. I eventually circled back to the same classroom toward the ending time of clinic. Truthfully, I had forgotten about the "off script" moment that had transpired earlier and thought nothing of just waltzing back into the same classroom with my attention-grabbing wardrobe. Upon entering, the boy stopped practicing his sight words and, as if on cue, said aloud, "Ew, why are you STILL wearing that pink shirt, mister? Didn't you go change?"

The second line from his Disney channel show script managed to break my teaching game face. I lost it by spilling out some giggles followed by several full-out guffaws, the kind of laughter reserved for a viral video of a kid saying something that is inappropriate, but is too darn cute so instead prompts a laugh as the video gains another "like." After letting my laughter escape, I put my game face back on, adjusted the curling upper lip itching to turn into a smile, and knelt down at eye level with this kindergartner. "Now remember what we talked about a few minutes ago. It's okay for boys to wear pink." Truthfully, I do not know if my message seeped in and, I must confess, this kindergartner had unintentionally managed to momentarily take me back to my own schooling days when I policed my own behavior.

I always knew I was different. The actual naming of my sexual identity as queer would come later as an adult, but I could self-articulate in my thoughts that I was just *different* from all the other boys. I dared not publicly claim this difference, choosing to instead push the difference away, stuff it away so deep I could not even conceive of a proverbial closet to stuff it away in, opting instead to lock it up and police it. I policed my mannerisms. I policed my speech. I policed my gaze. And yes, I even policed my attire. Ocampo (2013) documents this form of policing in his work on Filipino and Latino gay men who navigate their sexual identity within the context of the immigrant family. Referring to this form of self-policing as moral management, he explains this process as a form of "hyperconscious monitoring of gender presentation, behaviors and mannerisms, voice inflections, clothing choices, cultural tastes and even friendship networks" (Ocampo, 2013, p. 2) In my case, this moral management occurred as a kid. And now, here I was, a full-fledged adult and teacher educator, all eyes on me, maneuvering this organic teaching moment with finesse while secretly recalling earlier days when I dared not wear pink for fear it would give my queerness away. I ended up drawing attention away from the pink shirt, by grabbing for a picture book and engaged the kindergartner in a story instead.

A story helped me deflect the microaggression and now my own telling of the story with this kindergartner is helping me to speak on the subject of my identity as a Queer Chicano educator. Honing in on this particular story from my work as a teacher educator, allows me to illustrate why it matters to not only have diverse teachers and teacher educators, but specifically, also to have Queer Chicano educators disrupt the notion that teacher educators enter racial justice work from the same place. As a Queer Chicano educator, I teach from the Nepantla space – the in-between – and, as such, draw from this space to inform my approach toward education.

To elaborate, at the beginning of each semester I assign students an identity wheel exercise that requires them to unpack their respective identities. The assignment requires critical reflection and acknowledgment of privilege and/ or disadvantage when identifying with certain social identities. Responses are posted on a discussion board and students are required to respond to one another's assignments to stimulate thoughtful discussions while also building classroom community. Before students complete the assignment, I model the exercise in class, but present my identity wheel as a lecture, complete with projected photographs reflecting comments regarding the intersection of my identities. For example, when discussing social class, I situate my individual identity under class as part of my family's identity as members of the working class and intersect this identity in an immigration context. As I discuss this intersection of class identity, I project a photograph of my paternal grandfather's problematically labeled "Alien Laborer's Identification Card" from when he was a Bracero worker in the 1940s.

Of course, I also discuss my identity as a Queer Chicano and use this modeling exercise to come out to my students. Though I have been comfortably out for over a decade, every time I share this hybridity of identity to a new audience there is a sense of vulnerability I go through, especially when considering the backlash I have received in the form of heterosexist course evaluations. One such evaluation accused me of "making everything in the class gay." In spite of the potential risks of coming out during a lecture, the benefits outweigh any potentially damaging evaluation, especially when considering the countless queer students who instantly forge a connection of solidarity and consequently reframe the classroom as a safe space. I often see queer students don their own version of pink shirts by the next lecture because they feel their identities affirmed, visible, welcomed, accepted, and – most important of all – supported.

Yet another effective strategy I can impart involves the use of a visual tool I call an Intersectionality Matrix. This tool grew organically over years of teaching and originally was a visual I depicted on the board as a way to map out intersections of identity and to recognize the relationships such identities had with systems of power and theoretical frameworks that helped to analyze such systems. A colleague of mine, Dr. José Aguilar-Hernández, had a similar teaching tool to address the concept of third space, but he had it as part of a PowerPoint slide. I eventually transferred my scratches on the dry erase board over to a slide template he shared with me and I approximate its appearance in Table 15.1.

The actual visual I use has concepts which appear as I address them in my lecture. It also allows me to illustrate parallels between systems of power and acknowledge that multiple systems of power operate to oppress an individual or community who has intersecting identities that are positioned in the minority category. In addition to helping students understand intersectionality, I also use the matrix as an antiracist pedagogical strategy. I purposefully leave "Whites" and "people of Color" blank on the matrix until the very end. Before revealing them, I probe students for their thoughts on who should be listed in those categories and their rationales for their answers. In other words, I employ dialogic learning as inspired by Paulo Freire and informed by my intersectional positionality as a Queer Chicano educator.

Applying this approach requires placing five to six students in small discussion groups as I traverse the classroom observing their discussions before I open up the dialogue to a larger circle inclusive of the whole class. I make use of knowledge contextualized by my positionality to help build students' own content acumen by directing the whole-class discussion, peppering them with questions on how sexuality, gender, and class can

Table 15.1 Intersectionality Matrix

	Class	Gender	Sexuality	Race	Immigration Status
Social Locations	Lower Middle Upper	Womyn Transgender Muxeres Fa'afafine Men	Queer Lesbian Gay Bisexual Queer Challenged	Asian Black Indigenous Latina/o White	Undocumented Sin papeles Native Citizen
System of Power	Classism	Sexism	Homophobia? Heterosexism	Racism	Racist Nativism
Dominant Group (Privilege)	Upper Class	Men	Queer Challenged	Whites	Citizens
Minority Group (Oppressed, but Have Agency)	Working Class Middle Class Exploited Class	Womyn Transgender	Queers	People of Color	Undocumented Immigrants
Theoretical Frameworks	Social Reproduction Marxism	Black Feminist Thought Chicana Feminisms	Jotería Queer Theory	Critical Race Theory	LatCrit Borderlands Theory

intersect and inform race and racism. A salient example of this is the following set of questions I pose to students: "What happens to my male privilege when I am driving late at night in a predominantly White neighborhood and I get pulled over by a cop? In this context, does my gender work to my advantage or disadvantage when considering racial profiling?" This line of questioning allows for students to immediately apply intersectionality in their understanding of racism.

My lecture also addresses how power under each system governs who can experience the system as a member of a minority group and therefore oppressed versus who can be advantaged by the system as a member of a dominant group. I then make the matrix real for my students by situating myself and my own respective identities in the matrix. By doing this, I am able to share experiences on how intersecting systems of power operate to oppress queer Latinxs in general, specifically queer Chicanos in my case. For example, I offer comments on how the recent marriage equality movement has left out much-needed conversation about poverty in the queer Latinx community.

By sharing my own social locations first, when I get to the race component of the lecture, I often see head nods throughout the classroom as acknowledgment that connections are being made. At the risk of sounding like Oprah, students of Color and Whites alike have an "aha moment." This is underscored by students who typically share one of two responses reflecting such a moment of insight. For students who seldom engage in critical perspectives on race, their response can best be summarized as, "I finally understand racism as a system of power and can see how it can intersect with other forms of oppression." Students who are more developed in their critical race knowledge respond with, "I now have tools and language to help me articulate what racism means and how it operates while acknowledging an intersectional perspective." Of course, the actual words used by my students vary, but unpacking the nodding of heads and their immediate discussion comments, yields the two camps of transformative learning that takes place as a culmination of the lecture.

Without living in between, or in other words, as a Nepantlero, I doubt my strategies for antiracist teacher education would manifest itself in the way I have espoused in the classroom. To help bolster this claim, I turn to Anzaldúa (1987) yet again by offering another one of her concepts that breathes through my teaching – *La facultad*. In brief, *La facultad* is the capacity of the marginalized to see in surface phenomena the meaning of deeper realities, a form of sensing. It is this *facultad* that helps me to maneuver around the classroom, sometimes organically, with my Queer Chicano identity at the helm, sensing what to say, when to say it, how to say it, and planting seeds along the way with the explicit goal for those seeds to germinate throughout the semester and take root in antiracist dispositions for my students.

Once in a while, a seed surprises me in unexpected ways. Recently, I received a note scribbled on a self-reflection I have students write to assess their own participation in the class. The note read, "You wear your Queer

Chicano identity like a glove. It fits, it works, it educates. Thank you for a great semester." This brief, yet illuminating, note came from a student who also identifies as a Queer Chicano. His words further cemented my unapologetic commitment toward extending the dialogue of racial justice education to be inclusive of queer identities. Increasing the visibility of queer identities with respect to confronting racism not only helps move the dialogue forward, but also transforms the classroom. Coming out to students early in the semester is the first step toward increasing visibility. I then delve into my teaching toolkit – calling on Nepantla, lessons learned from wearing a pink shirt, enacting intersectional dialogues on racism – finessing these teaching experiences together to craft a community space for students to collectively confront racism.

Notes

1 I intentionally refrain from capitalizing most proper nouns and the first word of sentences due to the informal nature of the original social media post. This epigraph also employs a more creative writing voice and the lack of capitalization speaks to that type of writing. The few words I do capitalize are meant to stress the importance of those words within the context of the epigraph.
2 A shirt worn in certain regions of Mexico, Latin America, and now the US, that is characterized by its two rows of pleats running down the front and back of the shirt. The shirt is referred to as a *guayabera* because a traditional version of the popular shirt is adorned with a series of vertical open pockets on the front that were used to store *guayabas* (guavas) while picking them from the field. Subsequently, there has been a working class ethos associated with the shirt.

References

Anzaldúa, G. (1987). *Borderlands/La frontera: The new mestiza*. San Francisco, CA: Aunt Lute Books.
Ocampo, A. (2013). The gay second generation: Sexual identity and family relations of Filipino and Latino gay men. *Journal of Ethnic and Migration Studies. 40*(1), DOI: 10.1080/1369183X.2013.849567

Part IV

Pushing the Borders of
Teacher Education

16 Talking Race, Delving Deeper

The Racial Literacy Roundtable Series at Teachers College, Columbia University

Yolanda Sealey-Ruiz

Race, in the mind of many students, requires a verdict of innocence or guilt, identifies victims and criminals, and makes everyone either good or bad. And students work very hard to make their case so as not to be found "guilty", "criminal", or "bad."

(Guerrero, 2008)

At the close of the Summer 2008 semester, I wrote a message to the students who took my Teaching English in Diverse Social Cultural Contexts course. The letter I posted to the online platform was written to share my observations and feelings about how I experienced the class as their instructor. Although I later discovered that it was read by many of the students in a different way, my overall intent was to encourage them to continue developing their racial literacy skills. Below is an excerpt:

Dear Diversity Class:

As I think about our class this semester, it is impossible for me not to see each of you – each on your own journey toward becoming antiracist, culturally responsive educators – each at different places in this important journey. Some of you, in my opinion, have taken on the challenge of questioning what you believe you know about "others," and the best way to educate them. You have also taken an active stance in investigating what your role as an educator should be. Some of you, I believe, remain "stuck" in many of the ideas about "others" that you came into this class with, and still others of you I don't believe are ready to fully embrace self-examination and examination of society that will reveal to you that racism, privilege, and various social constructions prevent us from seeing our students as individuals; just as I have seen each of you this semester.

You have learned to write the things that you believe the professor wants to read, and you've learned to say things that appear you are moving forward in your thinking about these very complex issues, and then I read your Critical Conversation Group charts and journals, critical incident analyses, qualitative entries, and your first and final open letters, and I am reminded of the Hard and Heart work all of this requires. I am reminded of the better job that I must do in helping you see your Black and Brown students as "at promise" instead of "at risk."

The reality is, that not until many of you become the teacher-of-record in your own classrooms in what people call a "challenging school" will you think about some of discussions we tried to have in this class. Whether or not you even think twice about the texts we've read, the guest speakers we've had, the films you've seen, and the conversations you've started will depend on where you teach, how much support you receive, and how blatant the result of social inequity is in your school environment. I fear that for some of you, this class will have been and will remain a graduate course – and no more than that.

Be real with why you've chosen to teach. Be honest about why you have chosen to teach where you are teaching, and whom you are teaching. When you are completely honest about those questions, then you'll be getting somewhere in this struggle. Until this happens, you may just be performing...

Change toward others cannot occur until we examine our beliefs about ourselves in relation to others. Self-reflection and personal conviction about injustices that occur to other people are crucial first and second steps toward lasting change in how we view and treat people who are not like us.

Yours in the struggle,
Dr. YSR

As soon as I hit the "send" button on my computer, I felt deeply the risk that I had taken. It was a bold step for me as a Black female, untenured professor at this predominately White and wealthy institution to insist that race and racism be public topics for discussion. I wanted to bring the discourse started in my classroom that summer to a wider audience that included other teacher education students and clinicians. I also wanted young people to be a part of the conversation. I desired for the children my students served to engage in discourse that affected their lives in the classroom and society at large. Growing up as a Black girl in the South Bronx taught me to, as James Baldwin once wrote, "go for broke" in everything I had ever done. In other words, I was to live my life as though I had nothing to lose. To be sure, I had become so disheartened by many of my students that summer, I knew I had to "go for broke" and find a way to continue the conversation with them while bringing discourse on race and racism to the wider college community. It was in this spirit that the Racial Literacy Roundtable Series (RLRs) was born.

Reactions to the Letter

That semester, there were eighteen preservice teachers in the class who reflected some gender, ethnic, and racial diversity – three males and fifteen female students who self-identified as Black, Asian (Korean, Chinese), White, and Latino. I had convinced myself that they would be the perfect group to delve deep into conversations on the intersections of race, class, gender, ethnicity, and educational inequality. A few weeks after I posted the letter, I ran into Lauren, one of the White female students in the class. Before talking to Lauren that day, it was already clear to me that my students had read the letter as it had received 107 "hits" via the online system, but there were only three written responses. Lauren had spoken to many of the students and she explained that most of the students were offended by my letter and felt that I had "called them out" on racism. As a way to create an opportunity to discuss their reactions, I sent out an invitation for all of us to meet. The same three students who had previously responded to the original posting – Lauren, Emily, and James – were the only students who took up my invitation. For example, James, who is Korean American, connected to my letter by sharing that for many years he thought he was White, and that he was raised to believe that "whiteness" was something he should aspire to in life. He credited my Diversity class with challenging this thinking and helping him (re)embrace his traditional Korean cultural values. The three students and I became co-applicants on a Diversity grant. The grant provided $1,500 for food and facilitator honorariums, and in fall 2008 the first of the RLRs was facilitated by James. He brought along with him three of his fellow teachers and 15 of his middle school students.

The Concept of Racial Literacy

The concept of racial literacy is informed by scholarship that recognizes race as a signifier that is discursively constructed through language (Jhally & Hall, 2002); fluid, unstable, and socially constructed (Omi & Winant, 1986) rather than static; and not rooted in biology, but having "real" effects in the lives of individuals (Frankenberg, 1996). The architect of the concept of racial literacy, Harvard Professor Lani Guinier (2004), implores a shift from racial liberalism (considered a precursor to the Civil Rights Movement) to racial literacy, critiquing racial liberalism as an inactive, deficit approach to racial equality that subjugates Blacks to the position of victim and does not activate the required antiracist stance that Whites must take against their own racist ideals and actions. Racial literacy is a skill and practice in which individuals are able to probe the existence of racism and examine the effects of race and institutionalized systems on their experiences and representation in U.S. society (Rogers & Mosley, 2006; Sealey-Ruiz, 2011; Skerrett, 2011).

As it relates to teacher education specifically, teachers who develop racial literacy are able to engage in the necessary personal reflection about their racial beliefs and practices, and teach their students to do the same. Most teacher education graduates complete their programs without having experienced deep and sustaining conversations about race and how it impacts the teaching and learning process. When they enter their schools and classrooms they are not prepared to work with a diverse student body. A desired outcome of racial literacy in an outwardly racist society like America is for members of the dominant racial category (most of the nation's teachers) to adopt an antiracist stance and for persons of Color to resist a victim stance. Racial literacy in classrooms is the ability to read, discuss, and write about situations that involve race or racism, and apply this understanding to everyday living situations.

The RLRs

As an untenured professor, I took the risk of elevating the discussion of race and racism to a college-wide status because I felt it was that important. Although it took extra time to coordinate and administer the series because I did not have a graduate student to assist me, I felt an obligation to continue the conversation I had not been successful in having with my students that summer. I was frustrated with the majority of my students' resistance in acknowledging the impact of race on one's life chances. Since the creation of the Roundtables, there have been over 40 sessions presented by a total of 60 facilitators and nearly 800 participants in attendance. Facilitated by national scholars, master's and doctoral students, RLRs seek to cross community boundaries and promote intergroup communication, collaboration, and education. Past topics have included: The School-to-Prison-Pipeline, Racial Stereotypes and Labeling, Multiraciality, and Black Girls' Experiences in Schools.

To complement the multiple perspectives that are brought to the RLR forums, the material used to initiate discussions is multimodal and includes the use of literature, freewriting, spoken word, social media, and video. While difficult conversations do occur during the Roundtables, facilitators guide participants in building a respectful and supportive community in which participants feel comfortable sharing ideas and challenging each other's assumptions. In the tradition of how the series began, all facilitators write and offer a letter to RLR attendees. In this letter they share their journey to their chosen RLR topic. This approach embodies the notion that both youth and adults are bearers of and contributors to knowledge.

There are three specific goals of RLRs:

- *Encourage* attendees to question their assumptions about race, primarily, and other diversity issues; acknowledge and challenge their biases; and take a stance to actively resist racist and discriminatory practices, policies, and beliefs they may encounter in their teaching sites.
- *Engage* participants in critical conversations in a setting which encourages them to speak freely and openly about their hesitancies and concerns about teaching in urban settings.

- *Emphasize* reflexivity, and the re-examination of perceptions, and promote the idea of re-building a base for new perceptions founded on open-mindedness and understanding.

The Future of RLRs

Eight years ago when I began the RLRs my goals were modest. It was not until the third year of the series that I began to envision the RLRs as an opportunity for student activists to come together and resist the racism and injustice they witnessed (or perpetuated) in their student teaching and clinical sites. Initially, RLRs started as an attempt to continue the conversations I began with my Diversity class that one particular summer.

Since 2014, all Roundtable topics are dedicated to the lives of young people. Topics explore how race intersects with language and literacy practices, and explores the challenges to well-being for youth involved in foster care and/or the juvenile (in)justice system. For example, the first session of the 2013–2014 series was titled Possibilities of Designing with and for Underrepresented Communities: A Conversation about Participation, Court-Involved Youth, and Humility, facilitated by Tara L. Conley, a doctoral student who presented her original design of TXT CONNECT, a free mobile platform for court-involved youth living in NYC that allows users to access resources and information in their surrounding communities. During the 2014–2015 season, all six RLRs were focused on the topic of Youth, Education & Systems and for the 2015–2016 season, the topics of all RLRs take up the concept of Youth and Well-Being, which, for the first time, included high school students as RLR facilitators. For the 2016–2017 season, the RLR theme will be Youth Activism and all Roundtables will be conducted by middle, high school, and undergraduate students.

In 2016, at all three master's commencement ceremonies and a doctoral convocation, the President of Teachers College (TC), Columbia University highlighted the work of the RLRs. In her speech, she described the RLRs as a space at the college to talk about the rampant violence against Black bodies, to plan against injustices that plague schools and society, and for TC students to think through ways to interrupt the status quo of inequality and racism that characterizes our world.

The RLRs have been mentioned in the college's President's Report and featured on the college's website. It has received funding from the Dean and Provost's offices to both continue the Roundtables series and further develop college-wide racial literacy projects. I continue to develop projects that further the concept of racial literacy at my institution. My goal is to continue to encourage open, honest dialogue about race and racism and the way it plagues our institutions of learning and society writ large. It is significant for colleges of education to create spaces like the RLRs. Preservice and inservice teachers require spaces to openly discuss their biases and misconceptions about the students they are hired to serve. They also need spaces that can serve as a place of fellowship for them to figure out ways to shape their teaching into a pedagogy for liberation.

References

Frankenberg, R. (1996). *White Women, Race Matters: The social construction of whiteness.* Minneapolis, MN: University of Minnesota Press.

Guerrero, L. (2008). Pardon me, but there seems to be race in my education. In L. Guerrero (Ed.), *Teaching Race in the 21st Century: College teachers talk about their fears, risks, and rewards* (pp. 1–14). New York, NY: Palgrave Macmillan.

Guinier, L. (2004). From racial liberalism to racial literacy: Brown v. Board of Education and the interest-divergence dilemma. *Journal of American History 91*(1), 92–118.

Jhally, S., & Hall, S. (2002). *Race: The floating signifier* [DVD video]. Northampton, MA: Media Education Foundation.

Omi, M., & Winant, H. (1986). *Racial Formation in the United States: From the 1960s to the 1980s.* New York, NY: Routledge.

Rogers, R., & Mosley, M. (2006). Racial literacy in a second-grade classroom: Critical race theory, whiteness studies, and literacy research. *Reading Research Quarterly, 41*(4), 462–495.

Sealey-Ruiz, Y. (2011). Learning to talk and write about race: Developing racial literacy in a college English classroom. *English Quarterly. The Canadian Council of Teachers of English Language Arts, 42*(1), 24–42.

Skerrett, A. (2011). English teachers' racial literacy knowledge and practice. *Race, Ethnicity and Education, 14*(2). Routledge. Online DOI: 10.1080/13613324. 2010.543391

17 Creating Critical Racial Affinity Spaces for Educators

LaToya Strong, Margrit Pittman-Polletta, and Daralee Vázquez-García

Discussions about race and racism are silenced in teacher education programs and subsequently K-12 schools due to race-ignorant[1] practices and policies (Matias & Liou, 2015). Therefore, within schools, which serve to reproduce White hegemony (Jennings & Lynn, 2005), teachers are ill-equipped to deal with the reality of racism both inside and outside of the school system. This results in environments that make it hard for teachers committed to racial justice to make changes. As such, teachers committed to racial justice are cultivating and/or finding spaces outside of formal institutions to receive the training and support needed to address racism in education (Kohli, Picower, Martinez, & Ortiz, 2015). In New York City, The New York Collective of Radical Educators (NYCoRE), a grassroots, volunteer run collective, provides teachers with a critical space to address the racial inequities in school. Specifically, NYCoRE has two racial affinity groups that allow educators to convene around shared racial identities and "discuss dynamics of institutional racism, oppression, and privilege..." (Blitz & Kohl, 2012).

As Leonardo and Porter (2010) argue, and our experiences affirm, White people and people of Color (PoC) enter race dialogues from different positions. Thus, the needs of these groups in addressing racism, specifically in education, are radically different. In recognition of this, NYCoRE has two racial affinity groups, the Educators of Color Group (EoC) and the Antiracist White Educators Group (AWE-G), which provide space for teachers of Color and White teachers, respectively, to separately address their needs as teachers committed to racial justice. These spaces are not "safe spaces" (Michael & Conger, 2009) as safe usually denotes comfort for whiteness at the expense of PoC (Leonardo & Porter, 2010), but function as both communities and critical spaces that can lead to transformative change within NYCoRE, the education system, and throughout the communities served by each.

Historical Groundings

NYCoRE, part of The Network of Teacher Activist Groups (TAG), started in 2001 as part of the larger antiwar movement that developed after 9/11. NYCoRE began as a small group of teacher activists, with a majority of

---

PoC, who organized actions and developed curricula. In 2011 NYCoRE transitioned to a general membership structure, which resulted in a demographic shift to a majority White member body, mirroring the teacher demographic of New York City. Despite NYCoRE being a social justice organization, when new PoC attended NYCoRE member meetings they encountered the same dominance of whiteness present in their schools.

A sense of urgency emerged within the organization over the evident need for conversations about race, specifically in relation to the racial dynamics that had come to characterize member meetings. Subsequently, the core organizing body of NYCoRE and some of its more active members attended antiracism training and developed political education for the larger membership body centered on the intersection of racism and neoliberalism. In addition, two affinity groups were established. The first was the EoC founded in May of 2011 to address the concerns of members of Color and to cultivate a community in response to the predominance of whiteness in NYCoRE and education more generally. Also in 2011, NYCoRE held an Inquiry to Action Group (ItAG; Kohli et al., 2015) called My Classroom is Antiracist, which explored the dynamics of race and racism inside schools. The culmination of the ItAG and the formation of the EoC group prompted White members of the ItAG to form the Antiracist White Educators Group (AWE-G), to explore the role of White educators in antiracist work, and deepen members' understandings of racism and antiracism.

Although racial identity is at the forefront of each group's work, the methods used by each reflect the different needs of their members. Their differing practices have likewise evolved over time as each group has morphed to fit the needs of their respective communities. Accordingly, this chapter will outline some of the practices of each group and discuss how the two have collaborated. We begin by including the groups' mission statements, followed by a discussion of the ways in which each enacts its particular vision.

EoC Mission Statement

> Educators of Color (EoC) is a group of people who identify as educators of Color, who are committed to fighting for social justice in our school system and society at large. We emerged in order to uphold NYCoRE's commitment to maintaining majority people of Color. We seek to sustain a visible and critical presence within the larger NYCoRE collective. We advocate for a nurturing, transformative and action-driven space for educators of Color to connect, learn, struggle, and heal together. We do this work to build and connect bridges for our collective liberation.
>
> (NYCoRE Educators of Color, 2013)

Kohli (2016) has documented the racially hostile climates teachers of Color are subjected to in schools, which negatively impact their well-being as well as their retention. Within EoC we strive to create a supportive community to validate and reflect on these experiences in order to maintain our drive to teach. This environment allows us to unpack connections between educational and other institutional injustices as well as to discuss solutions to the myriad of injustices enacted upon teachers and students of Color. However, given that "person of Color" is a very broad and inclusive term, we acknowledge our different social positions and that historically our communities have had different relationships to whiteness and White supremacy. Thus, the space we create in EoC is necessarily intersectional and critical. Consequently, we challenge one another from a place of love to make our space truly transformative. We push our conceptualization of a liberated world past the limits imposed by White supremacy, so collectively we can bring our different lived experiences, histories, and imaginations into our shared community. We recognize that while we have extensive social justice work to do within and outside of education, showing up within EoC helps us clarify what we may or may not be ready to take on.

In teacher preparation programs, teachers of Color often feel isolated, excluded and deal with racist encounters that are a result of the institutional racism embedded in teacher education (Cheruvu, Souto-Manning, Lencl, & Chin-Calubaquib, 2015). This carries over to the classroom and school buildings where teachers of Color, and specifically members of EoC, have been pushed out of the classroom for teaching critical content or addressing injustices. To build a sense of community to negate isolation and negative encounters we make use of several methods of engagement to reach the EoC community. First, EoC is a non-hierarchical space where responsibilities are shared among members. We have specifically defined roles that members volunteer for on an annual basis, such as co-coordinators. We also have roles that are filled on a rotating monthly basis, like that of host and facilitator. Moreover, we use a revolving method for meetings, whereby the note-taker for one meeting becomes the facilitator of the next meeting. The result is that the equitable delegation of responsibilities creates a stronger feeling of belonging, as well as fostering a greater sense of ownership for the group as a whole.

We also build community through social media, having a presence on Instagram and Twitter, but it is through our Facebook page that we are most active. We use these platforms to share resources, curricula, and events related to education, race, and other marginalized identities. Unlike the other spaces in which we are present, these platforms are public and open to any person regardless of race. Our potlucks, listserv, and Google group, however, are reserved strictly for PoC. Due to the personal nature of some of the exchanges that take place in EoC, as well as the logistical planning that often occurs, we want this forum to be free of the White gaze (Yancy, 2008). This has been vital in our growth as social justice educators because EoC members have, in other spaces, had experiences in attempting to disrupt racism only to have the conversation derailed by White fragility (DiAngelo, 2011). Thus, EoC serves as a place of guidance and support for situations that arise in our educational settings since our schools do not have the support system or ability to address these needs.

AWE-G Mission Statement

The Antiracist White Educators Group (AWE-G) is an affinity group for White(-identified) educators seeking a critical space to examine and discuss race and Whiteness. The group's work is founded in reflection as action; critical reflection on our own racial identities allows us to build awareness of our role in perpetuating White supremacy. We keep race and racism at the forefront of our work together, because we are aware that as White people we can choose whether or not to engage in racial justice work.

(Antiracist White Educators Group, 2016)

AWE-G provides space for White educators to work in community toward developing a greater understanding of White supremacy, and our roles in either perpetuating or interrupting it within schools, relationships, and ourselves. At our monthly gatherings we cultivate community practices that invite White folks to process their insecurities and experiences, and pose questions so that we can enter into spaces we share with PoC without becoming defensive or guilty when dealing with issues of racism (DiAngelo, 2011). We study writings about White supremacy so we can see the insidious ways it shows up in our society and in our own behaviors; we share stories, troubleshoot problems, and role-play so that we can respond more effectively in moments when we say, do, or witness racist acts in the world. We strive to affirm and reclaim our culture (which White supremacy has robbed us of) for the purpose of cultivating positive White identities. We support and push each other to take more action in and outside of the classroom, in solidarity with PoC toward our collective liberation.

AWE-G gatherings are planned and co-facilitated by rotating partnerships and held in members' homes, where we break bread and get to work. We strive to include three foundational elements in every AWE-G gathering: Community Building, Education, and Action. This is based on the meeting structure of a fellow TAG group, the People's Education Movement-LA. Each month's co-facilitators determine the theme of the meeting and their methods of facilitation. Throughout the year, however, story circles are used to facilitate community building within the group. The story circle process involves telling stories around a circle, with each participant sharing a three-minute story on a given theme, followed by cross-talk, or dialogue, about the stories.

AWE-G members learned about story circles in 2011 from a pair of Teach for America (TfA) resisters at the Free Minds Free People Conference. The TfA resisters had been collaborating with veteran public school educators in New Orleans, who after Katrina and the corporate takeover of the city's schools, began organizing students, families, and teachers to try and reclaim the public education system. Telling stories, often about personal and professional encounters with racism, internalized racial superiority, or White privilege, allows educators to actively undo the White supremacist culture of individuality and heroism through the sharing of personal struggles and successes. Collective dialogue, or cross-talk, about the stories contextualizes our experiences within society, reinforcing awareness and understanding of our roles as gatekeepers of a racist school system, and moving us toward action.

Some actions members have taken include organizing book clubs around race-related texts, engaging in conversations around race and racism with friends and colleagues, planning and teaching lessons on race-related topics, and bringing antiracism trainings to their schools. AWE-G has also been working to increase our accountability to the larger NYCoRE community, which we see as a key component of our work in order to make our work transparent to the larger collective, to call in more White educators to the work, and to be actively in solidarity with EoC.

Conclusion

Although AWE-G and EoC operate as separate groups we also collaborate, notably through the planning and facilitation of workshops on race and racism in education. The presence of affinity groups has led to better understanding and inter-relationships between NYCoRE members participating in EoC and AWE-G. We believe that the ability of EoC members to stay in and fight for change in hostile educational environments, and of AWE-G members to engage in race dialogue without centering whiteness in a race-ignorant school system is because of the work that takes place within the affinity groups.

NYCoRE created these affinity groups out of necessity, due to the void of such spaces in teacher education programs and professional development. We believe it is imperative to foster a teaching force that is diverse, reflective of students, and culturally literate, to support and retain teachers of Color, and to push White educators to more effectively interrupt racist practices in schools. Teacher education programs can support this transformation through developing programs with a critical antiracist perspective that do not center whiteness or commodify the radical work being done in alternative spaces. To facilitate the development of such initiatives, teacher education programs must utilize the knowledge and experiences of teachers of Color (Kohli, 2009) and other antiracist teachers in establishing what the program needs to move toward an antiracist practice.

Note

1 We recognize the ableist manner in which "colorblind" has been used in race discourse and offer instead the term race-ignorant.

138   *LaToya Strong et al.*

References

Antiracist White Educators Group. (2016) *Mission*. Retrieved and adapted from https://sites.google.com/site/nycoreaweg/about-me

Blitz, Lisa V., & Kohl, B. G. (2012). Addressing racism in the organization: The role of white racial affinity groups in creating change. *Administration in Social Work*, *36*(5), 479–498.

Cheruvu, R., Souto-Manning, M., Lencl, T., & Chin-Calubaquib, M. (2015). Race, isolation, and exclusion: What early childhood teacher educators need to know about the experiences of pre-service teachers of color. *The Urban Review*, *47*(2), 237–265.

DiAngelo, R. (2011). White fragility. *The International Journal of Critical Pedagogy*, *3*(3), 54–70.

Jennings, M. E., & Lynn, M. (2005). The house that race built: Critical pedagogy, African-American education, and the re-conceptualization of a critical race pedagogy. *The Journal of Educational Foundations*, *19*(3/4), 15.

Kohli, R. (2009). Critical race reflections: Valuing the experiences of teachers of color in teacher education. *Race Ethnicity and Education*, *12*(2), 235–251.

Kohli, R. (2016). Behind school doors: The impact of hostile racial climates on urban teachers of color. *Urban Education:* 0042085916636653

Kohli, R., Picower, B., Martinez, A. N., & Ortiz, N. (2015). Critical professional development: Centering the social justice needs of teachers. *The International Journal of Critical Pedagogy*, *6*(2), 7–24.

Leonardo, Z., & Porter, R. K. (2010). Pedagogy of fear: Toward a Fanonian theory of 'safety' in race dialogue. *Race Ethnicity and Education*, *13*(2), 139–157.

Matias, C. E., & Liou, D. D. (2015). Tending to the heart of communities of color towards critical race teacher activism. *Urban Education*, *50*(5), 601–625.

Michael, A., & Conger, M. C. (2009). Becoming an anti-racist White ally: How a White affinity group can help. *Perspectives on Urban Education*, *6*(1), 56–60.

NYCoRE Educators of Color. (2013). Mission statement. *Educators of Color Group*. Developed at 2nd Annual Retreat, June 2013. Retrieved from http://www.nycore.org/projects/poc-group/

Yancy, G. (2008). *Black Bodies, White Gazes*. Lanham, MD: Rowman & Littlefield.

18 A People's Education Model to Develop and Support Critical Educators

Antonio Nieves Martinez

I feel so isolated in my school. Most of the teachers I work with are White and don't seem to feel a sense of urgency around serving our community. Because when I see my students, I see myself, I think I'm a lot more driven to support my students to develop a critique of oppression in society... I come to the inquiry group because there I'm surrounded by other teachers that can have this kind of conversation.

(Ms. Nieto, personal communication, n.d.)

In many schools, there is a disconnect between what teachers need for professional growth and the professional development they receive from their schools. Corcoran (1995) points out that the disconnect stems from a focus on one-size-fits-all, top-down models of teacher professional development that do not speak to the everyday realities of the classrooms. Exacerbating this problem, federal education reform policies mandate that professional development be aligned to state academic content standards, student achievement data, and standardized assessments (U.S. Department of Education, 2009).

Tired of professional development that did not respond to what she understood as the needs of teaching and learning in her classroom, Ms. Nieto, a high school English teacher, and community organizer, collaborated with a group of teacher-organizers from across Los Angeles County and co-founded the teacher inquiry group referenced in the interview excerpt above. Ms. Nieto expressed the urgency to support young people of Color with articulating an analysis of the ways their communities are positioned in the U.S. Ms. Nieto also expressed the difficulties of navigating a profession that largely views teaching as apolitical, which compounded her feelings of alienation and isolation. Through the continued political education she received as a community organizer, it became clear to her that it was important for the young people of Color in her classrooms to have access to a critical education. As such, in collaboration with other teacher-organizers, Ms. Nieto worked to create a teacher-led space for learning that supported them with bridging organizing work with their teaching practice.

Through their organizing experiences, these teachers were uniquely positioned to bring a sophisticated analysis of the ways oppression manifests itself in society. Developing a critical analysis of larger systemic issues fostered a willingness to work toward creating classrooms that speak to the realities of students and their communities. This chapter will examine the ways Ms. Nieto and her colleagues organized themselves during the 2012–2013 academic year to create a teacher-led space for learning that served as a place where teachers received support with navigating their classrooms, schools, and the larger teaching profession.

This teacher-led space for learning stems from the People's Education Movement, also referred to as People's Ed, a grassroots organization formed in 2012 made up mostly of teachers, graduate students, and community members of Color from across Los Angeles. While the goals of the organization are to honor the indigenous knowledges of the communities where members have lived and worked, the organizing efforts of People's Ed have been socially transformative because of the ways members are able to create a network of supportive, like-minded educators. As a group of critical educators, they believe education must work toward the liberation of communities of Color. In order to achieve the goal of liberation, and as a community organizing strategy to engage a broad base of educators, People's Ed have developed teacher-led spaces for learning, which I refer to as People's Led Inquiry (PLI). The PLI is a space facilitated by members of People's Ed and structured so that participants can interrogate their teaching with the goal of becoming skillful at creating classrooms that are community responsive. Over time, it has become apparent the PLI is more than teacher professional development. The PLI also serves as a space where educators are supported with navigating and surviving the oppressive conditions of their schools. In order to make explicit how the PLI has supported teachers, I draw from the organizing model of the Black Panther Party's Survival Program. I end this chapter with a brief description of the four tenets of the PLI.

Service for Surviving as a Critical Educator

> All of these programs satisfy the deep needs of the community but they are not solutions to our problems. That is why we call them survival programs, meaning survival pending revolution... So the survival programs are not answers or solutions, but they will help us to organize the community around a true analysis and understanding of their situation.
>
> (Newton, 2002, p. 230)

The survival programs created by the Black Panther Party (BPP) worked to address the immediate needs of the Black community and other oppressed peoples through free breakfast programs, health clinics, and services for prisoners and their families, to name a few, in order to engage communities in the larger struggle for justice (Hilliard, 2008). Huey Newton (2002) is clear that addressing the day-to-day needs of the Black community was not the immediate answer to changing larger systemic issues. However, supporting the Black community with meeting their day-to-day needs provided the opportunity to engage those community members with developing a critical analysis of the larger sociopolitical context of their experiences; developing a critical conscious is a necessary first step for social change.

In this case, the framework underlying the BPP's survival programs can be used to understand the PLI. The PLI provided teachers with the immediate support they needed to make sense of their working conditions while at the same time it supported them with creating an educational experience that was engaging, critical, and humanizing. For these teachers, survival meant dealing with the daily physical and psychological isolation that came with being critical of a system of schooling that reproduces the status quo. Teachers in the PLI were trying to make sense of "how" to survive a teaching profession that seemed to push out teachers that were critical of the kinds of educational experiences that low income Black and Latinx students received. Through the PLI, People's Ed advocated for teachers to develop the pedagogies that would better engage their students and in that process teachers created a space where they could be vulnerable about their struggles and triumphs. While the PLI does not immediately address larger systemic issues, it has served as an entry point into the organization for some; as a result, they have engaged in larger campaigns of the organization toward educational equity.

Four Tenets of a PLI

The PLI was a project of the Education Working Group of the organization and was attended by a broad range of educators (K-16) from a variety of disciplines. At first, the PLI was an attempt to address the gaps in the teacher professional development offered to teachers – pre-existing programs mainly focused on improving standardized test scores. The group met bi-weekly in a classroom in South Central Los Angeles, was teacher-led, and worked to develop inquiry questions that addressed colonization across content areas. The PLI meeting was divided into two parts: scholarly and applied. The scholarly segment consisted of the group discussing readings surrounding critical social theory, coloniality, and education. The applied aspect consisted of one participant presenting a problem of practice or curriculum to receive feedback from the group in an effort to improve the quality of their teaching.

Over the year, participation included nearly 30 educators, and meetings featured sustained dialogue and collaboration. It became apparent the PLI was more than teacher professional development. While it was a space to develop pedagogical and practical strategies, the PLI also became a place where teachers engaged in a dialectical relationship with one another; more broadly, they interrogated their work as educators working within a system of schooling. The multiple functions of the PLI can be described in the following four key tenets: Critical Praxis, Humanization, Solidarity, and Cooperation.

Tenet 1: Critical Praxis

In an attempt to develop their teaching practice, PLI members created a reading list grounded in cultural studies and colonialism that explored social, political, historical, economic, and educational theories. Group members chose readings they thought would support teachers in making sense of a macro/micro analysis of their positionality and the lived realities of students. The macro analysis afforded teachers with the lens to make sense of the complex social conditions under which they and their students live. This microanalysis provided participants a lens to understand the ways these complex social conditions impacted their classrooms and further deepened their purpose for teaching for social justice.

Tenet 2: Humanization

Freire (1970) describes humanization as the struggle to understand the conditions that make one oppressed and in that process see their humanity and that of others. The PLI was a place where teachers worked to understand systemic issues – namely schooling, colonization, and White supremacy – which engaged them in the process of humanization. This was especially important because teachers stated that they felt invisible at their school sites. In contrast, the PLI provided teachers the setting to meet, talk, listen, and challenge the isolation and alienation felt at their schools by developing caring relationships with other PLI participants as they worked to develop critical praxis.

Tenet 3: Solidarity

In previous work, I point to solidarity as a key aspect of People's Ed as a whole (Martinez, Valdez, & Cariaga, 2016); this notion holds true to the PLI space. The notion of solidarity relates to the varied ways people have relationships with others that are deepened because members of a community share certain beliefs, experiences, needs, and practices that are seen as integral to the community. In this respect, solidarity refers to how participants developed a sense of authentic kinship with one another. This notion of solidarity developed from a network of colleagues who held similar beliefs, cared for one another, and were committed to each other as they worked against systems that try to alienate teachers from one another and from their work.

Tenet 4: Cooperation

In other work (see Kohli, Picower, Martinez, & Ortiz, 2015), I point to the ways power is redistributed between participants and facilitators through Freire's (1970) dialogic action of cooperation. Cooperation suggests the importance of leaders working to shift the power dynamics with those they serve in order to come together in authentic dialogue to develop a collective revolutionary consciousness (Freire, 1970). From here, cooperation, as a dialogic action, entails teachers working together to create spaces for learning that more closely reflect the holistic needs of their students and themselves. Creating a space where educators can engage in the dialectical process of cooperation was mediated through authentic dialogue where participants were engaged as *subjects*, rather than objects, as they struggled for liberation.

Conclusion

The PLI participants illustrate the importance of preparing teachers to understand teaching as a political act. Teachers can no longer enter the profession thinking they are free of bias, apolitical, or neutral. Instead, teacher education programs must encourage preservice teachers to examine their social locations as starting points from which to ground their teaching practice. An exploration of identities and social context must not be relegated to one social foundations course but instead should undergird entire programs. Educators have the potential to bring about social transformation when they organize themselves to challenge dominance while also teaching in the interest of the communities they serve.

PLI members demonstrated their refusal to merely accommodate state-sanctioned guidelines related to teaching and curricula. Instead, PLI members strove to create the kind of learning spaces they want for their children, students, and communities. Educators need not depend on state-sanctioned mechanisms for developing, supporting, and sustaining critical educators, especially critical educators of Color. Perhaps most importantly, in that process of transforming education for teachers, PLI members modeled an important aspect of building the capacity of teachers – along with their students and their communities – to be leaders.

References

Corcoran, T. B. (1995). *Helping Teachers Teach Well: Transforming professional development*. New Brunswick, NJ: Consortium for Policy Research in Education.

Freire, P. (1970). *Pedagogy of the Oppressed*. New York, NY: Continuum.

Hilliard, D. (2008). *The Black Panther Party: Service to the people programs*. Albuquerque, NM: UNM Press.

Kohli, R., Picower, P., Martinez, A. N., Ortiz, N. (2015). Critical professional development: Centering the social justice needs of teachers. *International Journal of Critical Pedagogy, 6*(2), 7–24.

Martinez, A. N., Valdez, C., & Cariaga, S. (2016). Solidarity with the people: Organizing to disrupt teacher alienation. *Equity and Excellence in Education, 49*(3), 300–313.

Newton, H. P. (2002). Black capitalism re-analyzed I: June 5, 1971. In D. Hilliard & D. Weise (Eds.), *The Huey P. Newton Reader* (pp. 227–233). New York, NY: Seven Stories Press.

U.S. Department of Education. (2009). *Race to the Top Program: Executive summary.* Retrieved from www2.ed.gov/programs/racetothetop/executive-summary.pdf

19 Freirean Culture Circles as a Strategy for Racial Justice in Teacher Education

Cati V. de los Ríos and Mariana Souto-Manning

As two of the few Latina teacher educators in a predominantly White university, we have rejected acultural notions of quality in education. While literature is increasingly signaling the need for clearer articulations of a pedagogy of teacher education, meaning a pedagogy of teaching teachers (Goodwin et al., 2014; Zeichner, 2005), we concur that as a profession we must continue to think deeply about this question through a racial equity lens. Valuing the lived experiences of minoritized communities (McCarty, 2002), like those to which we belong, and recognizing the fact that many teacher educators express that they lack pedagogical preparation (Goodwin et al., 2014), we were drawn to Freirean culture circles as a necessary approach to teacher educating. Culture circles as a framework for critical pedagogy (Souto-Manning, 2010) in teacher education afford participants the opportunity to emphasize the democratic positioning between teachers and learners (Freire, 1970). As teacher educators, culture circles have also provided us with an entry point for critical discussions around racial (in)justice, a topic that is often absent within the lexicon of teacher education.

We believe that the preparation of individuals for critical thinking and activism in a democratic society should be at the center of teacher education. Following Freire's vision of education, teaching must include the identification of a community's "funds of knowledge" (Moll, Amanti, Neff, & Gonzalez, 1992) and then use such resources to both influence and develop pedagogies. This is in contrast to the overwhelming number of teacher education programs that employ Freire's (1970) banking concept of education where "the transmission of knowledge to students' brains [is] like money into banks" (Souto-Manning, 2010, p. 11). This effectively positions teachers as passive and ahistorical recipients of knowledge. Hence we recognize the need to problematize traditional teacher education pedagogies, which includes challenging the racial inequalities rooted in the curricula and pedagogies of teacher education.

Freire's work urged us to move from the all-too-common transmission of knowledge toward the co-constructing of a critical pedagogy of teacher education (Freire, 1970). This chapter outlines how we approach Freirean culture circles as a strategy for cultivating critical literacies of racial (in)justice with teachers and communities. We do so from the situated perspectives of Latina teacher educators who "dare teach" (Freire, 1998) within a context that remains markedly White (Sleeter, 2001) and too often maintains racialized power relations (Evans-Winters & Twyman Hoff, 2011). Furthermore, as cultural workers (Freire, 1998) committed to racial justice, we collectively concur that "no one knows it all; no one is ignorant of everything" (p. 39) and that we are all on a journey of becoming (Freire, 1970).

The university classrooms we enter are packed with symbols that suggest that teachers have full power. These rooms include chalkboards for writing "correct" answers, desks that face one speaker, and tall podiums that gaze down on sitting students. These conditions are not only predictably replicated in K–12 classrooms, but are also racialized – in New York City, urban public school teachers tend to be White, whereas their students often come from communities of Color. As teacher educators of Color, we asked how we could disrupt this student–teacher power dynamic, and how we could provide young people, as well as members of the communities they come from, a sense of ownership over their own education.

Freirean culture circles provided a model to source themes from the community and a framework to guide critical and democratic discussion. But the model itself does not create an actual physical space of equity – we knew that we had to move off campus and choose a time that would honor working families and also educators. We decided that Saturday mornings in the heart of Harlem was a space to remove "formal power" from teachers and situate our work in a place where students and families of Color felt empowered. Participating teachers shed their symbols of power – they traded their laptops for cups of coffee and their formal demeanors for hugs and laughter. Together, through our culture circle series, we propose that the challenge of teacher education is to (re)position teachers as "transformative intellectuals" (Giroux & McLaren, 1996). Such (re)positioning requires deliberate resistance to hegemonic practices that continue to position teachers as technicians who transmit knowledge to their students (Giroux, 1988) and toward seeing themselves as "cultural workers" (Freire, 1998) who learn from and alongside the communities they serve.

A Brief Overview of Freirean Culture Circles

Having each previously facilitated culture circles inspired by Freire's work within our own P-12 classrooms and on campuses in the context of teacher education, we decided to collaborate through a culture circle series open to the public. The primary objective of culture circles is to encourage *conscientização* (Freire, 1970), which Freire defines as a critical meta-awareness of participants' social and material conditions (Souto-Manning, 2010). Critical meta-awareness can be facilitated by the critical questioning of such conditions through dialogue. Freirean culture circles are grounded on the premise that "...no educational experience takes place in a vacuum, only in a real context—historical, economic, political, and not necessarily identical to any other context" (Freire, 1985, p. 12).

Culture circles are grounded in two fundamental tenets: a) education is a political process; and b) critical dialogue is an essential process of educating and education. These tenets occur within the learners' social and political contexts. As the participants' social realities and conditions are problematized critically and politically, critical dialogue is engaged as a means to identify the root cause(s) and collectively create solutions to those problems (Souto-Manning, 2010; 2011).

While there are well-known aspects to culture circles, there is no one way to participate in culture circles and they need to be reinvented as they arise in different social contexts (Souto-Manning, 2010). Culture circles start with an investigation of generative themes, meaning topics of grave social importance to those participating, whereby the facilitator learns from the communities of which participants are members. From these investigations, themes are identified and positioned at the center of the curriculum. These generative themes are often codified, meaning they are visually represented. While Freire used codifications such as photographs and song lyrics, we found videos particularly effective. Then, in culture circles, facilitators and participants engage in critically reading a text and problematizing it, learning from each other through dialogue, problem solving, and envisioning ways of positioning themselves as agents of social change (whether individually or collectively).

Adapting Freirean Culture Circles to a New York City Context

After a long week in the classroom, teachers often spend their weekend sleeping in, replenishing, and engaging in non-work-related activities. Despite the stressful and physical demands of teaching, an overwhelming number of educators from across the New York City area willingly woke up early on Saturday mornings, navigated the intricacies of the subway system, and made the trek to Harlem for monthly culture circles. Many of the teachers arrived with their colleagues ready to engage in this "extra" intellectual work because they felt these culture circles covered social themes that were important yet too often missing from their traditional teacher preparation programs.

Along with preservice teachers, we invited local high school students, P-12 teachers, community members, and teacher educators. As "cultural workers," we studied the social contexts in which New York City teachers, students, and families co-existed (Freire, 1970; Souto-Manning, 2010) to identify important themes experienced by the community. We followed what was trending on social media and drew from those issues for discussion topics at the culture circles. Prominent topics were then characterized into a theme and represented in flyers inviting the community to participate in dialogue to collectively problematize the theme in question. These flyers were distributed via grassroots organizations and social media.

Over periods of no less than two hours, we sought to problematize the socially constructed oppressive realities through discussion circles. We learned alongside one another. We encouraged participants to take the stance of both a teacher and a learner as we sought to blur those normative roles ourselves (Freire, 1970). In this context, culture circle participants (including ourselves) negotiated their roles as agents of change (as indicated by spoken comments and written evaluative comments). Culture circle participants saw themselves as facilitators of learning and also as those who problematized learning (Souto-Manning, 2011).

The generative themes selected and explored in the culture circles series represented some of the most pressing and oppressive issues for students and educators in New York City. Some of the culture circles explored the impact of high-stakes testing, undocumented youth identities and rights, LGBTQ youth empowerment, and neoliberal education policies affecting working class communities of Color. These generative themes all came from community members (often through social media). While we hosted the culture circles, we made sure that members of the greater grassroots community served as facilitators to honor community voices and lived experiences.

Culture Circles in Action: "Exploring Stop-and-Frisk in NYC"

One culture circle, led by New York City educators Judy Pryor-Ramirez and Claire Sternberg focused on students' in-school and out-of-school experiences with "Stop-and-Frisk" policies. As reported by The Leadership Conference on Civil and Human Rights (2011), New York Police Department (NYPD) officers repeatedly engage in Stop-and-Frisk practices that are racially biased and promote racial profiling. Blacks and Latina/os are reported to be stopped-and-frisked by NYPD officers at an alarmingly disproportionate rate compared to Whites in the city. Furthermore, the use of excessive physical force by NYPD officers on Blacks and Latina/os during this procedure also occurs at significantly higher rates compared to that of Whites. This inconsistency "exists despite corresponding rates of arrest and weapons or contraband yield across racial lines" (p. 11). These practices are well known and were pervasive under the administration of former New York City Mayor Bloomberg. We decided to focus on this topic because both Judy and Claire felt that there were limited spaces to discuss, engage, and organize with other educators around the severity of this issue as it relates to youth of Color.

The culture circle on critically problematizing Stop-and-Frisk lived experiences was kicked off by videos, which codified the counternarratives of male youth of Color who had been dehumanized by Stop-and-Frisk policies. These videos were found on the Open Society Foundations website (https://www.opensocietyfoundations.org/) titled, *Kasiem Just Wants to Move Freely without Fear* and *This Is Not What I Became a Cop for*. So that participants would have some background knowledge about the history of Stop-and-Frisk in New York City schools, prior to coming to the culture circle, they were asked to read selected chapters of reports provided by the New York Civil Liberties Union.

To begin the culture circle, facilitators Judy and Claire invited participants to listen and learn from the video clips. It was through the reading of the larger macro context (the report) and the acknowledgment of everyday dehumanizing storied experiences (the videos) that participants problematized what they were seeing and experiencing in their local schools and communities. Furthermore, participants attempted to situate the issue(s) within their own lived realities while addressing and troubling the roots of the problem.

Implications for Teacher Education

The various stakeholders of the culture circles learned from and with each other through dialogue. They collectively envisioned transformations and took up different actions in their own communities. For several educators, these culture circles served as a catalyst to organize and participate in some of their first political marches and protests against zero-tolerance policies. Other teachers made promises to be more vocal on their campuses around the disproportionate disciplinary actions across racial and socioeconomic lines. And almost all of the participating educators began to consider ways of incorporating such troubling yet pervasive issues (e.g. racial profiling) into their classroom curriculum, building more robust vocabularies and critical analysis skills, and thus better preparing their students to combat the realities many of them experienced day in and day out. Regardless of the action they each decided to take up, all of the participants thought more explicitly about how teachers like themselves are implicit in this problem – and about their responsibility to do something about it. These divergent actions highlight how valuable it is for preservice teachers to sit side-by-side with community members – including high school students – and learn from the reservoirs of knowledge beyond our universities' walls.

Using culture circles in our formal and informal teacher education contexts pushed us to identify the need of a critical pedagogy of teacher education. The implications of our practice reaffirm the need for a pedagogy of teacher education that disrupts racial inequality and positions teacher educators humbly as learners. And while we recognize that culture circles will have to be recreated and reinvented across contexts rather than simply "imported" (Freire, 1998), we propose that Freirean culture circles can serve as a framework for envisioning a critical pedagogy that moves teacher education beyond ivory towers by including community members and by centering on community issues of equity and racial justice.

References

Evans-Winters, V. E., & Twyman Hoff, P. (2011). The aesthetics of white racism in pre-service teacher education: A critical race perspective. *Race, Ethnicity and Education, 14*(3), 461–479.

Freire, P. (1970). *Pedagogy of the Oppressed.* New York, NY: Continuum.

Freire, P. (1985). *The Politics of Education: Culture, power, and liberation* (D. Macedo, Trans.). South Hadley, MA: Bergin & Garvey.

Freire, P. (1998). *Teachers as Cultural Workers: Letters to those who dare teach.* Boulder, CO: Westview Press.

Giroux, H. (1988). *Teachers as Intellectuals: Toward a critical pedagogy of learning.* New York, NY: Bergin & Garvey.

Giroux, H., & McLaren, P. (1996). Teacher education and the politics of engagement: The case for democratic schooling. In P. Leistyna, A. Woodrum, & S. Sherblom (Eds.), *Breaking Free: The transformative power of critical pedagogy* (pp. 301–331). Cambridge, MA: Harvard University Press.

Goodwin, A. L., Smith, L., Souto-Manning, M., Cheruvu, R., Reed, R., Tan, M., & Traveras, L. (2014). What should teacher educators know and be able to do?: Perspectives from practicing teacher educators. *Journal of Teacher Education, 65*(4), 284–302.

Loughran, J. (2008). Toward a better understanding of teaching and learning about teaching. In M. Cochran-Smith, S. Feiman-Nemser, & J. McIntryre (Eds.), *Handbook of Research on Teacher Education: Enduring questions in changing contexts* (3rd ed.) (pp. 1177–1182). New York, NY: Routledge.

McCarty, T. (2002). *A Place to be Navajo: Rough Rock and the struggle for self-determination in Indigenous schooling.* New York, NY: Routledge.

Moll, L., Amanti, C., Neff, D., & Gonzalez, N. (1992). Funds of knowledge for teaching: Using a qualitative approach to connect homes and classrooms. *Theory into Practice, 31*(2), 132–141.

Sleeter, C. E. (2001). Preparing teachers for culturally diverse schools: Research and the overwhelming presence of whiteness. *Journal of Teacher Education, 52*(2), 94–106.

Souto-Manning, M. (2010). *Freire, Teaching, and Learning: Culture circles across contexts.* New York, NY: Peter Lang.

Souto-Manning, M. (2011). A different kind of teaching: Culture circles as professional development. In V. Kinloch (Ed.), *Urban Literacies: Critical perspectives on language, learning, and community* (pp. 95–110). New York, NY: Teachers College Press.

The Leadership Conference on Civil and Human Rights. (2011, March). *Restoring a National Consensus: The need to end racial profiling in America.* Washington, DC: The Leadership Conference on Civil and Human Rights. Retrieved from http://www.civilrights.org/publications/reports/racial-profiling2011/racial_profiling2011.pdf

Zeichner, K. (2005). Becoming a teacher educator: A personal perspective. *Teaching and Teacher Education, 21*, 117–124.

20 The Institute for Teachers of Color Committed to Racial Justice

Cultivating Community, Healing, and Transformative Praxis

Marcos Pizarro

I finally feel like I'm not the only one. This is the first time in a long time that I don't feel crazy. I needed this space to heal from the constant assault on my intellect and spirit that I have experienced as a teacher.[1]

In our work at the Institute for Teachers of Color Committed to Racial Justice (ITOC), my colleagues and I have heard words like this shared by teachers of Color who span the entire country. From small towns in the South to rural communities in California, and from the urban schools of Philadelphia, New York, Chicago, Los Angeles, and Oakland Asian American, African American, Latina/o, and Native American teachers have shared these same feelings. Working in public schools and being committed to racial justice demands a constant battle against a dominant racial ideology built on the deficit framing of communities of Color, feeding on a steady diet of unacknowledged racial microaggressions, and resulting in the undermining and often failure of both students and teachers of Color.

ITOC, an intensive professional development offered each summer, exists to support teachers of Color who strive to use their vocation to help youth, schools, and communities of Color to succeed in school and achieve racial justice. It was developed to address the reality that teacher education does not prepare teachers for this work and that there are few, if any, professional development opportunities built around racial justice (Brown, 2014). For six years, ITOC has centered racial justice research and approaches to schooling and organizing to affirm, support, and enhance the transformative work of teachers of Color. ITOC's unique focus requires that participants have an advanced racial literacy and an assets-based approach to working with students of Color (assessed through an application that all participants must complete). This design is a response to the fact that there are many teachers, including teachers of Color, who are not ready, nor willing, to confront the dominant racial ideologies in the schools and communities in which they work. While supporting teachers who need the opportunity to develop basic levels of racial literacy is important, it is not part of the work of ITOC. The benefit of focusing on teachers with an assets-based, advanced racial literacy is that it allows us, the ITOC organizers, to deeply support these teachers who seek a space in which they do not have to take the inordinate amount of time required to expose the role of White supremacy to those who refuse to acknowledge its dominance in U.S. schools. Being immersed in an environment in which the radical, racial justice epistemology of teachers of Color is centered transforms these teachers' relationship to their vocation (Kohli & Pizarro, 2016).

Dominant racial ideologies that demean the intellectual abilities and contributions of teachers of Color and their students are so pervasive and deeply woven into the fabric of daily school practice that teachers of Color with a commitment to racial justice find themselves feeling like they are the crazy ones. They work in a "racial matrix," where the intergenerational inertia behind dominant racist ideologies and their corresponding policies and practices make it invisible to those who accept our current, dramatic racial inequality as natural. This is reflected in the reality that K-12 schools continue to focus on the achievement gap, without acknowledging the education debt (Ladson-Billings, 2006). It is experienced by teachers of Color in charter school networks and Teach for America, both of which emphasize a commitment to reducing educational inequality without recognizing the fundamentally racist underpinnings of their focus on addressing the supposed deficits of communities of Color. The racial matrix is embodied by the countless progressives in schools who define themselves as allies to communities of Color, but who nurture the popular discourse that disparages students, families, and communities, rewarding teachers and students who do the same.

The hidden role of White supremacy in schools is like the air we breathe, unseen and unacknowledged but a fundamental and necessary part of life as it is. This is the racial matrix in which racial justice-minded teachers of Color find themselves, which is why they come to ITOC. Despite the strengths they bring to the classroom, teachers of Color committed to racial justice are challenged as troublemakers and incompetent (Kohli & Pizarro, 2016). Isolated and unsupported in their schools, these teachers of Color often do not have the tools to confront this complex set of forces.

These opening paragraphs deliberately paint a harsh image of the experiences of teachers of Color committed to racial justice in 2016. This portrayal mirrors the angst, anxiety, turmoil, and spiritual anguish that teachers of Color share with us every summer. When they join us at ITOC, they often spend at least two days unloading, finally exhaling after holding their breath for nine months, having tried their best to avoid the toxic air hanging in the halls of their schools. These teachers seek a space where they can breathe and heal, but also acquire the tools and the community they need to return to the racial matrix and help both their students and colleagues actually see it, deconstruct it, and begin to transform and transcend it.

Since our challenge to mainstream racial understanding is so severe, we strive to make ITOC a space fundamentally distinct from other professional development opportunities for teachers. It is focused on: 1) community building, 2) racial justice healing, and, 3) praxis-oriented tools for confronting and transcending the racial matrix.

Community Building

Given the isolation that so many of the ITOC teachers experience, building a community of peers and mentors who share an advanced racial literacy is essential to their persistence in the profession. This sense of community is achieved in a number of ways. Working groups create an intentional community for ITOC teachers that lasts long after the summer, often with the teachers staying in contact and offering support throughout the next school year. Social media becomes a mechanism for maintaining this sense of community with many sharing ideas, questions, and opportunities related to racial justice practice in schools.

Meals are shared and teachers are encouraged to get to know each other and to build on the conversations initiated in different sessions. A community dinner is held at a local restaurant, as well as an after-hours social gathering at another local venue, leading to ongoing informal community building throughout ITOC. In addition, different artists (poets, singers, comedians, and storytellers) share their work with the group, and the affirmations this provides the teachers as a collective help concretize their sense of connectedness. Finally, and many teachers say most importantly, we have a DJ who plays music throughout ITOC, always finding a way to bring the teachers together, often choosing songs that remind them of their shared commitment to racial justice, and at other times just making them bob their heads as a community, creating a sense that racial justice work does feel good.

Each year, we are struck by the sense of community that develops in just three days and when we close our circle at the very last session, giving everyone the chance to exchange goodbyes with each person, the time this takes clearly reflects the meaning of our collective to the teachers. For many, the interracial nature of this newly formed community is truly transformative. Many of our teachers come from and teach in areas that are heavily dominated by one racial group. Becoming connected to other teachers from regions that they often know nothing about provides a new sense of community that is revelatory. Recognizing that the racial justice work they are pursuing is connected to that of colleagues who teach Filipino students in San Francisco, Mexican American students in Phoenix, African American students in Baltimore, and other communities across the country solidifies their sense of purpose and challenges the isolation they are made to feel in their schools. A critical component of the ITOC approach is that teachers recognize that their racial justice work has to be done in community, even when they may be the only teacher with a commitment to racial justice in a given school. We want them to understand that the racial matrix thrives on teacher isolation and so the racial justice planning that they complete at ITOC includes their ongoing consultation with other ITOC participants, as well as racial justice colleagues and allies wherever they find them.

Racial Justice Healing

Each year, ITOC begins as a space into which teachers of Color from around the country step cautiously. Accustomed to conventional professional development opportunities that preach equity but support practices that maintain and even further inequity, these teachers are well versed in disappointment. As we demonstrate our engagement with racial justice practice by grounding ITOC in the most compelling and visceral racial issues of the moment (such as institutionalized racial violence, racial battle fatigue, and the erasure of the epistemological power of teachers of Color in our schools), a sense of relief and comfort sets in. Often, in the first day or two of ITOC, we find that teachers begin to relax, let their racial guard down, and share their challenges. Inevitably, the teachers highlight the liberation of not feeling that they are crazy (referenced in the opening), as they often feel in the schools in which they teach whenever they challenge "normal" school practices that demean and disenfranchise students and communities of Color.

The stories that teachers begin to share as ITOC continues reveal the impact that the racial matrix has on them. As we have found through our research with the ITOC participants, many are experiencing racial battle fatigue (RBF) (Pizarro & Kohli, forthcoming; Smith, 2004; Smith, Yosso, & Solórzano, 2006; Smith, Allen, & Danley, 2007). The incessant drumbeat of dominant ideologies that reinforce White supremacy through school policy and practice have intellectual, emotional, spiritual, and physiological effects on teachers of Color. These teachers so often have to approach their daily entry into the school as if they are preparing for battle, strapping on their emotional and intellectual armor to protect themselves. Over the course of weeks, months, and then years, the effects of this struggle can be severe. For this reason we have approached our work as a practice of racial justice healing. We acknowledge the racial matrix, recognize the effects it has on them, and provide them the opportunity to build a community of support that affirms both their strength and their right to access that support (something that many have no outlet for in their daily lives). Specifically, we: 1) share a racial justice framework that affirms their experiences (such as highlighting the way that "Whiteness as property" [Harris, 1993] shapes school practices), 2) encourage them to share their stories as part of our work to continually develop the framework through the eyes and daily experiences of teachers of Color, and 3) provide specific workshops that center healing as a vital part of effective racial justice teaching (e.g. Nurturing Critically Compassionate Classrooms: Integrating Trauma and Healing Informed Strategies with Students of Color). We encourage them to understand this healing process as ongoing work in which they must always be engaged as part of a community and which they can begin to model for and with their students and communities.

Praxis-Oriented Tools for Confronting and Transcending the Racial Matrix

The racial justice healing practices of ITOC are powerful for the teachers, but to pursue their racial justice goals in their schools, they need and seek concrete tools that can be used in their daily practice at any number of levels.

Each year, after reviewing the teachers' applications and the challenges and needs they identify, we design a set of praxis-oriented tools that teachers can apply to specific aspects of their jobs. These are integrated into keynote presentations from racial justice leaders who bring their research and experience to the teachers. In addition, we plan four sets of workshops that complement the keynotes and organizers' sessions and hone in on specific needs of teachers (considering topics from racial justice curriculum development to teacher organizing, and from restorative justice practices to creative writing for student healing and growth). Finally, we integrate working sessions in which the teachers organize in groups around themes that are most pressing to them. These groups integrate the tools acquired in the rest of ITOC and end with well-mapped plans to address their focal issues with both timelines and identified support people to help them achieve their goals.

The explicit focus on nurturing praxis-oriented tools in a multi-tiered process provides racial justice-minded teachers with a support system for pursuing their goals through realistic strategies, practices, and daily habits. Embedded in a culture of transformation in ITOC, the teachers who work with us appreciate both this pervasive shift in their thinking about their practice and the focus on how they can sustainably confront and counter the racial matrix in which they teach.

Conclusion

Actively working for racial justice in the U.S. today demands a commitment to struggle for the rest of our lives. It also typically results in a feeling that our sanity is being questioned and often directly challenged by our colleagues and supervisors. ITOC was created to address these realities and provide an ongoing space in which racial justice-minded teachers of Color can be supported in a community that provides them with praxis-oriented tools to help them find healthy ways of sustainably pursuing racial justice.

Sadly, these are not objectives that are shared in teacher education. Each year, ITOC participants reference the fact that we provide the training that they wished they had in their teacher education programs and in their ongoing professional development opportunities. The reality is that teacher education typically lives so deep inside the racial matrix that those responsible for it do not see the ways in which the dominant paradigm defines even their efforts to be racially conscious. Furthermore, so many ITOC participants describe battles with instructors and administrators in teacher education, who rather than providing a space for them to explore the critical issues described here, challenge their perspectives, belittle their contributions, and compound the effects of RBF. Teacher education programs that truly hope to confront racial inequality have to earnestly unpack the racial matrix, their role in it, and the fact that White supremacy has been ignored in their programs in ways that lead excellent and much-needed teachers of Color to feel that they are crazy.

Note

1   Through the project described in this chapter, we have collected narratives from hundreds of teachers. They cover many themes. I have summarized the most prevalent themes in this opening.

References

Brown, K. D. (2014). Teaching in color: A critical race theory in education analysis of the literature on preservice teachers of color and teacher education in the U.S. *Race, Ethnicity, and Education, 17*, 326–345.

Harris, C. I. (1993). Whiteness as property. *Harvard Law Review, 106*, 1709–1791.

Kohli, R., & Pizarro, M. (2016). Fighting to educate our own: Teachers of Color, relational accountability, and the struggle for racial justice. *Equity and Excellence in Education, 49*, 72–84.

Ladson-Billings, G. (2006). From the achievement gap to the education debt: Understanding achievement in U.S. schools. *Educational Researcher, 35*, 3–12.

Pizarro, M., & Kohli, R. (forthcoming). Racial battle fatigue among racial justice-minded teachers of Color. Manuscript in preparation.

Smith, W. A. (2004). Black faculty coping with racial battle fatigue: The campus racial climate in a post-civil rights era. In D. Cleveland (Ed.), *A Long Way to Go: Conversations about race by African American faculty and graduate students* (pp. 171–190). New York, NY: Peter Lang.

Smith, W. A., Allen, W. R., & Danley, L. L. (2007). "Assume the position … You fit the description": Psychosocial experiences and racial battle fatigue among African American male college students. *American Behavioral Scientist, 51*, 551–578.

Smith, W. A., Yosso, T. J., & Solórzano, D. G. (2006). Challenging racial battle fatigue on historically white campuses: A critical race examination of race-related stress. In C. Stanley (Ed.), *Faculty of Color Teaching in Predominantly White Colleges and Universities* (pp. 298–327). Bolton, MA: Anker Publishing Company.

21 Growing Our Own Hope

The Development of a Pin@y Teacher Pipeline

Edward R. Curammeng and
Allyson Tintiangco-Cubales

10 Years Later, a Letter

Dear Pin@y Educational Partnerships (PEP) Family and Friends,

"Liberation is thus a childbirth, a painful one."

Although this is one of my favorite quotes from Paulo Freire's *Pedagogy of the Oppressed* (1970) one of the major texts that informs our work in PEP – it has become clear to me that *childbirth* may not be an appropriate allegory for *liberation*. After ten years of being part of PEP and having birthed my own child, I began to realize that childbirth is only the beginning of liberation. It is really about the *raising* of a child, of children, of youth, and of people that more accurately represents the process of liberation, a protracted struggle. PEP's past 10 years have been a *Political*, *Emotional*, and *Purposeful* process of liberation, a process of raising a community, a critical community.

Even when PEP began in fall 2001, our goals were already "political." We as Filipinos in the United States, did not see ourselves in history books, in teachers, administrators, leaders, or even in the media. But we saw our high drop out rates, depression, suicides, economic hardship, and all the violence in our neighborhoods and in our homes. We could see the hate against Filipinas/os, between Filipinas/os, and within ourselves. We could see that Filipinas/os and similarly marginalized peoples were suffering on the global, local, and personal levels. It was clear that our communities needed hope.

Along with our "political" agenda to transform education, PEP has been an "emotional" journey. Every year our PEP *barangay* grows. And every year more and more people call PEP home. In this "political" and "emotional" home that we have built together, our work has become increasingly "purposeful." Our purpose goes beyond teaching methods and creating lesson plans and beyond simplistic multicultural activities and culturally relevant pedagogy. Our purpose is about *liberation* beyond *childbirth*. Our purpose is to *raise a community*, a community of people who are willing to commit themselves to social justice, a community of people who are willing to do what it takes to transform our lives.

Salamat!
Ate Allyson
October 2011

Pin@y Educational Partnerships: Emergent Critical Pin@y Teachers

The letter that opens this chapter was written by co-author and Pin@y[1] Educational Partnerships (PEP) founder, Allyson Tintiangco-Cubales, dedicated to the PEP community commemorating PEP's 10 years of "growing our own hope." In 2001, PEP began as a mentorship program connecting undergraduate and graduate students from San Francisco State University's (SFSU) Asian American Studies Department with students at Balboa High School in the Excelsior neighborhood of San Francisco. PEP's presence at Balboa was in response to increasing tensions between Philippine-born and U.S.-born Filipina/o students. PEP would soon emerge as a program serving Pin@y students and students of Color throughout San Francisco public schools and a space to grow Pin@y teachers. Each year over 50 undergraduates and graduate students from SFSU and neighboring Bay Area universities serve as PEP teachers in local K-12 schools, colleges, and universities. In many ways, PEP has grown a generation of teachers. While not a formal credentialing program, PEP teachers receive invaluable preparation and experience teaching in PEP classes rooted in critical pedagogy and ethnic studies. Said differently, the partnership supports its teachers to teach in PEP K-college classes.[2] Because of their diverse teaching experiences within the partnership, dozens of PEP teachers have decided to formally pursue K-12 teaching. Many have identified nuances in the training they received with PEP compared to their respective teaching credential programs. In this chapter, we draw from the experiences of former PEP teachers that have gone on to earn their teaching credentials to share how PEP exists as a Pin@y teaching pipeline counter to formal teacher credentialing programs.

Producing PEP: Strategies for Preparation, Practice, and Praxis

Much of PEP's success as an ethnic studies teaching pipeline is in large part due to the commitment of the roughly 60 PEP teachers who serve the PEP community each year. PEP was built to embody "barangay pedagogy." In Tagalog, *barangays* are small communities or political units. The word *barangay* is derivative of *balangay*, small boats used by Malay settlers to navigate the islands that would later become the Philippines. Philosophically a barangay can mean, "we are all in the same boat" or "the people in a barangay are in the struggle together, for better or worse" (Tintiangco-Cubales, Daus-Magbual, & Daus-Magbual, 2010). Thus, a driving force of PEP has been to respond to the lack of Filipina/o American teachers most apparent in schools with large Filipina/o student populations. The four R's of PEP's goals are: 1) to *Retain* both Filipina/o high school and college students, 2) *Recruit* high school students to pursue college and recruit college students to pursue careers in education, 3) *Reflect* on the historical and contemporary experiences of Filipina/o Americans, and 4) Provide *Research*, training, and service-learning opportunities for students and PEP teachers.

Prior to the start of the school year, PEP teachers participate in a weeklong intensive teaching institute known as *Tibak*, a riff on the Tagalog word *aktibista* or activist. PEP teachers read texts including: *Pedagogy of the Oppressed* (Freire, 1970), *Teaching to Transgress* (hooks, 1994), and *Theatre of the Oppressed* (Boal, 1993). Teachers also read interdisciplinary texts like *Little Manila is in the Heart: Making of the Filipina/o American community in Stockton, California* (Mabalon, 2013) and *Coming Full Circle: The process of decolonization among post-1965 Filipino Americans* (Strobel, 2001). These texts, among others, serve as the theoretical foundations for projects including: youth participatory action research (YPAR), teacher participatory action research (TPAR), and PEP's Community Show (see Tintiangco-Cubales, Daus-Magbual, Desai, Sabac, & Torres, 2016).

After each PEP class, teachers engage in a process of reflection to think through their pedagogy, consider how they could have supported themselves and their students better, and reflect on how the lesson was received by PEP students. Additionally, PEP teachers attend weekly meetings at SFSU where they practice teaching their lesson plans in front of their peers. This exercise provides productive feedback for the teachers themselves, but also encourages collaboration to strengthen their craft as educators. PEP teachers reflect on their teaching as well as the relationships and connections they develop with their barangay and the students they serve.

PEP teachers are usually pre-credential apprentices (though some do come into PEP with their teaching credential) who gain experience conducting research, designing, developing, and teaching critical Filipina/o American and ethnic studies in teams otherwise known as *barangays* (Tintiangco-Cubales et al., 2014). In barangays, PEP teachers gain skills through the practice of critical pedagogy, curriculum development, lesson planning, and teaching (Tintiangco-Cubales et al., 2010). More often than not, barangays are comprised of PEP teachers with varying years of teaching experience, research interests, and content backgrounds. It is worth noting, our teacher pipeline now includes several former PEP students that have become PEP teachers themselves. Aileen Pagtakhan, a middle school history teacher in the Bay Area and former PEP middle school teacher shared,

> The Barangay teaching prepared me that we do not do this work alone. It took a while to build community in the cohort... PEP has prepared

me to value the practice of collaboration with others and practice providing and taking feedback.

(A. Pagtakhan, personal communication, March 14, 2014)

In this way, the barangay is at once a symbol and source for community building and collaboration former PEP teachers have found useful bringing into their respective credential programs. For our teachers that have gone to pursue their credentials, the barangay is a resource and network where they can return, find support, resources, and reflect on their purpose as teachers. The PEP barangay is a sustained and intergenerational community where teachers have a space to share, learn, grow, and reflect.

Raising Pin@y Teachers

A hallmark of PEP is how it prepares, develops, and raises its teachers. PEP's approach to teacher preparation counters mainstream teacher education in a number of ways. First, traditional teacher training lacks a critique of education and theoretical discourses (Darling-Hammond, 2006). However, PEP poses problems encountered in education beginning with teachers' own schooling experiences and is infused with theoretical discourses that include critical theories and pedagogies informed by ethnic studies. Eduardo Daza Taylor, an after-school hip-hop studies teacher in Los Angeles and former PEP high school teacher offers:

> I feel that the best way to learn something is to simply do it. One can read all the readings, do all the research, understand all the theories, but until that person steps into the classroom, he or she will never know what it is like to be a teacher. In my credential program, I felt that there was a huge gap between theory and practice. We studied so much theory but would hardly see it in practice because we were not given the spaces or because the faculty would not always model it. Part of it comes from the credential programs being under a university system. PEP is from the ground up – by the people for the people. It is pure and organic.
>
> (E. Taylor, personal communication, March 31, 2014)

Second, teacher training's fetishization with methods and the development of extrinsic motivation breeds capitalist sensibilities most apparent in high-stakes testing and the standardization of education. PEP prepares teachers to focus on praxis, the connection between critical content, method, purpose, and reflection. This focus builds intrinsic motivation toward engaged learning by developing students' abilities to read the word and their worlds and demonstrates how PEP teachers integrate rigor with critical content to disrupt the false binary that the two are unrelated. Third, teacher education programs overwhelmingly present ahistoricized and generalized strategies to address student problems evoking deficit framings of students of Color. PEP, however, operates from the vantage of historical/social contexts with a deep and complex understanding of how social toxins and inequity are structured. This is achieved by learning through a decolonizing lens that develops agents of social justice and critical hope (Duncan-Andrade, 2009). Verma Zapanta, a high school world history teacher working in Koreatown, Los Angeles and former PEP high school coordinator, had this to share:

> There is also a huge disconnect between the academy and the community in my credential program. My teacher ed program requires student teachers to work in partnership schools in underprivileged, low income areas, yet the majority of faculty who are advisors in our program have little to no experience working in those very same communities... With PEP, the teaching pipeline is seen from K-college and bridging the community with our schools is a top priority.
>   (V. Zapanta, personal communication, March 30, 2014)

Fourth, mainstream teacher education programs often conflate "social justice," "diversity," and "multiculturalism" while maintaining White supremacy, heteropatriarchy, and metanarratives of salvation as status quo for teacher education. PEP is interdisciplinary, drawing from ethnic and Asian American studies, critical race and queer studies, history, Pinayism,[3] and women of Color feminisms. Verma Zapanta's reflection described the necessity for embodying and practicing social justice. She said, "In my program, social justice education is an idea that is theorized and remains in the classroom. In PEP, social justice is grounded in the community, it is practiced every day" (V. Zapanta, personal communication, March 30, 2014). Finally, as research has increasingly demonstrated, teachers of Color often experience the individualistic and hierarchical nature of teacher preparation through tropes like the "master teacher–teacher student" binary (Achinstein, Ogawa, Sexton, & Freitas, 2010; Jackson & Kohli, 2016). PEP disrupts the oppressive nature of this by viewing all teachers as students and students as teachers.

Hope, Growth, Change: Teaching Pipelines Reimagined

Paulo Freire reminds us of the transformative capacities of education to change people. Indeed, PEP has changed because of the people involved, and arguably PEP has transformed education. Teacher education programs can learn from how PEP has developed a deep commitment to serving people and reimagining what preservice teachers and teacher education's needs are. What is more is how we think about what a teaching pipeline and teacher education *should* be. Therefore we posit the following reflections for ourselves and others to consider when growing their own hope: how might teacher education transform to incorporate ethnic studies concepts and approaches for all preservice teachers? What role do hope, love, and activism have in shaping teacher preparation? In what ways might a barangay approach to teacher education be useful for novice teachers? How can we better support and continue developing teacher educators' knowledge? These are but a few meditations we think about in this work. With collective agency and reflection we continue to grow hope for future Pin@y teachers and teachers of Color.

Notes

1   Pinay/Pinoy are nicknames for Filipinas/os in America, adopted by some of the earliest Filipina/o immigrants to Hawai'i and the United States. Pin@y is a gender-neutral term to include both Filipina/o males and females, popularized by Pin@y students at UC Berkeley in the 1990s.
2   At the elementary level, PEP offers Filipina/o American studies and during regular instruction PEP teachers collaborate with Filipino Foreign Language for Elementary School teachers to support language learning. At the middle school PEP is offered as an elective. PEP high school classes are California A–G approved and eligible for college credit.
3   See Tintiangco-Cubales, A. G. (2005). Pinayism. *Pinay Power: Theorizing the Filipina/American experience*, 137–148. and Tintiangco-Cubales, A., & Sacramento, J. (2009). Practicing pinayist pedagogy. *Amerasia Journal, 35*(1), 179–187.

References

Achinstein, B., Ogawa, R. T., Sexton, D., & Freitas, C. (2010). Retaining teachers of color: A pressing problem and a potential strategy for "hard-to-staff" schools. *Review of Educational Research, 80*(1), 71–107.
Boal, A. (1993). *Theatre of the Oppressed.* New York, NY: Theatre Communications Group.
Darling-Hammond, L. (2006). Constructing 21st-century teacher education. *Journal of Teacher Education, 57*(3), 300–314.
Duncan-Andrade, J. M. (2009). Note to educators: Hope required when growing roses in concrete. *Harvard Educational Review, 79*(2), 181–194.
Freire, P. (1970). *Pedagogy of the Oppressed*, trans. Myra Bergman Ramos. New York, NY: Continuum.
hooks, b. (1994). *Teaching To Transgress.* New York, NY: Routledge.
Jackson, T. O., & Kohli, R. (2016). Guest editors' introduction: The state of teachers of color. *Equity and Excellence in Education, 49*(1), 1–8.
Mabalon, D. B. (2013). *Little Manila is in the Heart: The making of the Filipina/o American community in Stockton, California.* Durham, NC: Duke University Press.
Strobel, L. M. (2001). *Coming Full Circle: The process of decolonization among post-1965 Filipino Americans.* Giraffe Books.
Tintiangco-Cubales, A., Daus-Magbual, R., & Daus-Magbual, A. (2010). Pin@y educational partnerships a counter-pipeline to create critical educators. *AAPI Nexus: Asian Americans and Pacific Islanders Policy, Practice and Community, 8*(1), 75–102.

Tintiangco-Cubales, A., Daus-Magbual, A., Desai, M., Sabac, A., Torres, M. V. (2016). Into our hoods: Where critical performance pedagogy births resistance. *International Journal of Qualitative Studies in Education*.

Tintiangco-Cubales, A., Kohli, R., Sacramento, J., Henning, N., Agarwal-Rangnath, R., & Sleeter, C. (2014). Toward an ethnic studies pedagogy: Implications for K-12 schools from the research. *The Urban Review*, 1–22.

About the Editors

Dr. Bree Picower is an Associate Professor at Montclair State University in the College of Education and Human Development. She was awarded the Scholar Activist of 2013 by the Critical Educators for Social Justice Special Interest Group of the American Educational Research Association. Her last book, a co-edited collection of essays called *What's Race Got to Do with It? How current school reform maintains racial and economic inequality* is available from Peter Lang Publishers. Her first book, *Practice What You Teach: Social justice education in the classroom and the streets*, explores a developmental continuum toward teacher activism. She has taught in public elementary schools in Oakland, California and New York City. Resources and publications affiliated with her work can be found at www.usingtheirwords.org and she can be reached at picowerb@montclair.edu.

Dr. Rita Kohli is an Assistant Professor in the Education, Society and Culture Department in the Graduate School of Education at the University of California, Riverside. She is Co-Founder and Co-Director of the Institute for Teachers of Color Committed to Racial Justice (ITOC) and former Chair of the Critical Educators for Social Justice Special Interest Group of the American Educational Research Association. A former Oakland Unified School District teacher and teacher educator, Kohli has spent over 15 years in urban public schools across the country. Her research interests include race, racism and K-12 schools, teacher education, teachers of Color, critical race theory in education, and school racial climate. Her scholarship has been published in academic journals such as *Urban Education, Teacher Education Quarterly*, and *Race, Ethnicity and Education*, where she serves on the editorial board. Dr. Kohli can be reached at rita.kohli@ucr.edu.

About the Contributors

Mari Ann Banks (Roberts) is an Associate Professor of Multicultural Education and Director of the Master of Arts in Teaching program at Clayton State University (CSU). She is Director of CSU's Center for Academic Success and works with multiple education advocacy organizations. More information about her work can be found at her website www.docmari.com. The author wishes to thank Louis, a dynamic young man who will make a difference.

Patrick Roz Camangian, PhD is an Associate Professor of Teacher Education at the University of San Francisco and has been a high school English teacher since 1999. Camangian honors the tradition of teacher research, applying critical pedagogies in urban schools. His areas of expertise include: critical pedagogy, critical literacy, culturally empowering education, and socially transformative teacher development.

Noemí Cortés is an educator whose special interest in teaching has centered on language development and diversity. She has taught children of Color, inservice teachers, and preservice teachers at graduate and undergraduate levels. Additionally, she has worked as a coach of inservice and preservice teachers, curriculum specialist, and administrator. She would like to thank her mentor and friend Cecily for her support and feedback, her parents for being her first models of racial justice warriors, and her partner Ayenew for his love and guidance.

Edward R. Curammeng is a PhD candidate in Education at the University of California, Los Angeles. In his research, he uses critical race theory to examine the relationship between Education and Ethnic Studies for students and teachers of Color. He is a former Ethnic Studies teacher with Pin@y Educational Partnerships. Edward and Allyson would like to thank the students, families, and teachers of Pin@y Educational Partnerships. Past, present, and future. *Tatlong Bagsak!*

166 About the Contributors

Cati V. de los Ríos is an Assistant Professor in the Education, Society and Culture Program in the Graduate School of Education at the University of California, Riverside. Informed by her experiences as a school teacher, her research explores Chican@/Latin@ adolescents' literacy practices and their participation in high school Ethnic Studies courses.

Alison G. Dover is an Assistant Professor in the Secondary Education Department at California State University, Fullerton. Alison's recent publications include *Preparing to Teach Social Studies for Social Justice: Becoming a renegade* (Teachers College Press) and articles in *English Journal*, *The Educational Forum* and *Journal of Adolescent and Adult Literacy*. It takes a village to write a chapter. This one would not be the same without the challenges, suggestions, and push-back from Brian Schultz, Bree Picower, and Rita Kohli. Thank you!

Sameena Eidoo holds a PhD in Curriculum Studies and Comparative, International and Development Education from the University of Toronto. She has developed and taught courses focusing on educational equity and justice for teacher education and is the recipient of the Graduate Excellence in Teaching Award from Western University. She would like to thank Iman, Amber, Tatiana, and Michaela for their courageous teaching, and Kari Dehli and Jillian C. Ford for encouraging her to share her counterstories through this collection. She would also like to thank Angela MacDonald-Vemic for her acts of solidarity, and Amrah Salomon for her insightful comments on earlier drafts.

Jillian Carter Ford is an Associate Professor of Educational Equity at Kennesaw State University in Kennesaw, Georgia. Dr. Ford's teaching, research, and community involvement centers on equity literacies, Black feminist studies, and decolonial studies. Her out-of-work passions include reading, utilizing snail mail, laughing, and engaging in warm-weather outdoor activities. She sends many thanks to Erika Meiners, Therese Quinn, and Karyn Sandlos for supporting her early on and thanks also to the Queer & Trans People of Color communities in Atlanta who have aided in her recovery and rebirth.

Dr. Daren Graves is an Associate Professor at Simmons College. In addition to his teaching duties, Dr. Graves serves as the liaison between Simmons College and the Boston Teachers Union Pilot School (BTU School) where he coordinates professional development opportunities for the BTU School staff, coordinates the placement of Simmons interns, and works directly with BTU School students. The author would like to thank his immediate family and the many communities of Black folks (past and present) whose strong shoulders support him and propel him to fight the beautiful struggle.

Tyrone C. Howard is a Professor of Urban Schooling and Associate Dean of Equity and Inclusion at the Graduate School of Education and Information Studies at the University of California, Los Angeles. He also serves as the Founder and Director of the Black Male Institute.

Harper Benjamin Keenan is a doctoral candidate in Curriculum and Teacher Education at Stanford University. Prior to pursuing his PhD, Harper taught elementary school at Community Roots in Brooklyn, New York. He offers thank yous to Peter for his openness to sharing our story, to all of his students for their constant inspiration, and to Bree and Rita for their incredible mentorship through the writing process.

Eduardo Lara is a Sociology Lecturer at California State University, Long Beach. He has also taught in the field of Teacher Education at universities throughout Los Angeles. His research interests include the militarization of schools, Latino education, queer perspectives in learning, and pedagogical implications of student resistance as political activism. He is grateful to the queer community of Color for inspiring his work. As familia, we dare to be different while navigating life from the world of Nepantla. He writes for us, to us, and about us.

Dr. Tanya Maloney is an Assistant Professor in the Department of Secondary and Special Education at Montclair State University. She entered education as a mathematics teacher and Teach For America corps member in Chicago. Her research focuses on issues of race, racism, and equity in teacher education.

Antonio Nieves Martinez is an Assistant Professor in the Social Justice Education Concentration at the University of Massachusetts, Amherst. His research interests include critical and culturally relevant pedagogies, critical professional development for K-12 teachers, youth participatory action research, teacher organizing, and education for liberation. He would like to thank People's Ed, Ms. Nieto, and HTZN for the continued support and inspiration.

Alana D. Murray, PhD, is an educator activist who taught world history, U.S. history and currently serves as an Assistant Principal. She is Co-Editor, with Jenice View and Deborah Menkart, of *Putting the Movement Back into Civil Rights Teaching*. Dr. Murray serves as the Co-Coordinator for the Equity and Excellence certificate. She would like to thank her co-coordinator, Heather Yuhaniak, and her husband, Khalif Blue, for their unwavering support.

Sonia Nieto is Professor Emerita of Language, Literacy, and Culture, University of Massachusetts, Amherst, and has devoted her professional life to issues of equity, diversity, and social justice. She is the author of 11 books and has received many awards for her scholarship and advocacy, including six honorary doctorates. In 2015, she was elected a member of the National Academy of Education. Dr. Nieto would like to thank all the students she was privileged to teach over her long career and the many mentors who believed in her, as well, of course, as her husband and family. Without them, this – and everything else she has written – would not have been possible.

Margrit Pittman-Polletta worked as a special education elementary school teacher for seven years in NYC public schools. She worked with the New York Collective of Radical Educators (NYCoRE) as a core member and co-facilitator of the Antiracism White Educators Group. She offers thanks to the NYCoRE community for being down for struggle with courage and love toward our collective liberation.

Marcos Pizarro is a Professor in Mexican American Studies at San José State University. He coordinates MAESTR@S, a social justice organization that develops and implements a transformative education model with Latin@ communities, and works with schools on the development and implementation of Latinx Studies curricula to enhance Latinx student engagement. He is also the Co-Coordinator of ITOC. He would like to thank the Co-Directors of ITOC, Rita Kohli and Rebeca Burciaga for allowing him to be part of this amazing collaboration. Many thanks to the ITOC community across the country who are true racial justice warriors.

Dr. Yolanda Sealey-Ruiz is an Associate Professor of English Education at Teachers College, Columbia University. Her research interests include racial literacy, culturally responsive pedagogy, literacy and urban school environments. She is founder and faculty sponsor of the Racial Literacy Roundtables Series at Teachers College.

Mariana Souto-Manning, PhD, is an Associate Professor of Education at Teachers College, Columbia University. She is a former preschool and primary grades teacher. As a teacher educator, she teaches courses related to early literacy, multicultural education, and critical pedagogy. From a critical perspective, her research examines the sociocultural and historical foundations of early childhood teacher education, early schooling, language development, and literacy practices in pluralistic settings, and focuses on issues of racial and cultural justice.

LaToya Strong is a scholar educator activist. She is a doctoral student in Urban Education at the City University of New York Graduate Center. She is a former NYC public school science teacher and a member of NYCoRE. She offers many thanks and much love to the Educators of Color Group!

Joanne Tien is a PhD candidate at the University of California Berkeley. Her research centers around critical pedagogy, democratic citizenship, and movements for social change. Her work is influenced by her involvement in queer women of Color communities, and labor, feminist, and racial justice movements. Prior to graduate school, Joanne taught elementary school. She offers many thanks to Daniel Perlstein, Kris Gutiérrez, Rebecca Tarlau, and Christyna Serrano for their support and reading of this work; and special thanks to all her students, from whom she has learned so much.

Allyson Tintiangco-Cubales, PhD, is a Professor in the College of Ethnic Studies at San Francisco State University. In 2001, she founded Pin@y Educational Partnerships (PEP), an Ethnic Studies educational pipeline that creates partnerships and projects that work toward social justice. She is also the Co-Founder of Teaching Excellence Network and Community Responsive Education.

Daralee Vázquez-García is a public school Spanish teacher and Adjunct Lecturer of multicultural/bilingual education at Brooklyn College. She is a long-standing teacher activist member of NYCoRE. Daralee thanks all the members of NYCoRE, LaToya, Margrit, and her son Gianni.

Heather E. Yuhaniak is an educator activist, doctoral student, and district-level equity specialist whose interests include multicultural teacher education, racial identity development, and White antiracism. She is Co-Founder and Coordinator of both a graduate certificate and master's program in Equity and Excellence in Education. Heather wishes to thank her husband and children for supporting her scholarship and night/weekend activism and her partner-for-life, Alana Murray, for her friendship, inspiration, and invitation into our beloved community.

Index

End of chapter notes are denoted by a letter n between page number and note number.

Forgiveness

1. Giving up my right to ___
for the offense... It is not denying
the offense

2. Releasing my right to ___ it
is not releasing the need for justice

3. Letting go of ____ it is not

4. Dependent on ____ not on the
other person

5. Freedom... it is not
necessarily